Italy From a Backpack

Italy
FROM A
Backpack

Edited by
Mark Pearson and Martin Westerman

Europe From a Backpack
www.europebackpack.com

Requests for permission should be addressed to:
Pearson Venture Group
P.O. Box 70525
Seattle, WA 98127-0525
U.S.A.

For more information, visit www.EuropeBackpack.com

Cover design and graphics: Greg Pearson
Copy editing and page layout: Tracy Cutchlow

Library of Congress Cataloging-in-Publication Data
Pearson, Mark (Mark R), 1980—
Westerman, Martin (Martin), 1950—
Italy from a backpack. – 1st ed.
p. cm. -- (Europe From a Backpack Series)

ISBN (10): 0-9743552-4-0
ISBN (13): 978-097435524-5 (paper)
1. Italy—Description and travel.
2. Pearson, Mark. 3. Westerman, Martin.
Library of Congress Control Number: 2006932742

To my mom and dad,
who introduced me to Italy

CARTOLINA POSTALE

When preparing to travel,
lay out all your clothes
and all your money.
Then take half the clothes
and twice the money.
- Susan Heller

LE PIÙ BELLE TERME DEL MONDO
SALSOMAGGIORE
PERIODO DI CURA
MARZO — NOVEMBRE

stories

roma

cinque terre

firenze & toscana

authors

stories, *con't*

Introduction

ask any traveler to Europe's "Boot" *(lo Stivale)*, "Why Italy?" and he or she responds with the almost inarticulate bemusement of someone in the infatuation phase of a love affair. Italy is irresistible. We return again and again for the cuisines, the wines, the festivals, the unique regions and attitudes—all rooted in the very soil under the traveler's feet.

If you live in the West or speak any Romance or Germanic language, you can trace roots back to here, in the Roman and Greek Empires, even if you're not Italian. Your diet probably depends in part—or entirely—on Italian cuisine: pizza, spaghetti and meatballs with parmesan and crusty garlic bread, minestrone, mineral water, Caesar salad (invented in Florida, actually, but since it's named after Caesar...) and gelato. You may have salivated over Ferraris and Lamborghinis; perhaps you appreciate Italian style and the composure with which Italians approach life. They may promptly finish their midday espressos standing at narrow, high-top tables, but Italians will take three or four hours to enjoy a dinner that doesn't begin until at least 8 p.m. Ah, simple pleasures.

Italy From a Backpack is full of pleasures, too—stories of young people whose discoveries make delightful, even surprising reading. My co-editor, Mark Pearson, hatched this idea for books about youthful European travels when he returned home from studying art history in Rome and backpacking around Europe. He found that people weren't so interested in viewing his 2,200 digital photos. Instead, they wanted to hear great stories.

At the time, few, if any, books of stories were written by and for backpackers—even though, every year, nearly two million Americans ages

18 to 29, and hundreds of thousands of Brits, Canadians and Australians, head for Europe to travel, study and work. Most carry their worldly possessions on their backs, travel on shoestring budgets, and decide daily where they'll go and what they'll do. Often, these free-ranging nomads experience marvels that elude people who carry suitcases and make reservations.

Mark put out an invitation on the Web for stories, and the rest, as they say, is history. The series includes *Europe From a Backpack*, *Spain From a Backpack* and, now, *Italy From a Backpack*.

So, join us as we find Reine Bouton, fresh from Metairie, Louisiana, attempting to imitate Italian female attitude in "High Heels From Hell," and Bill Fink hitting a snag as he tries to catch a morning bus for Rome in "Hostage of the Hostile Hostel." We find as many reasons to travel here as there are backpackers. They come for history ("Not As Seen on TV"), family ("Finding Signora Bacca"), study ("Layering"), romance ("The Way of Love"), adventure ("Shirts Off for Bill and Ted"), art ("Art Appreciation") and exploration ("Ligurian Daydream"). Generally, travelers head first for the three must-see cities, Rome, Florence, and Venice, and branch out from there. One section in this book is devoted entirely to Cinque Terre, because backpackers are raving about this string of five coastal villages on the Italian Riviera, featured in Rick Steves' guidebooks.

While guidebooks are useful, telling us where to go and what to do, stories about what people experienced are powerful. The better they're told, the more we feel as if we are participating in them ourselves. Accompanying Heather Strickland in "Not As Seen on TV," we are told that no guidebook could have revealed Pompeii to her the way discovering it on her own did. She writes, "The Discovery Channel couldn't come close to (describing) the overwhelming feeling of walking through streets where once-vivacious people died running for their lives. The slideshows and pictures could never explain this place."

At a time when we're bombarded by the Internet, social-networking sites, all means of media, overwhelming life details, and bizarrely focused news that transfixes us in horrified fascination, it's lovely to break away and transport ourselves, however briefly, to other places, where good things happen, we gain wisdom, and everything turns out all right.

The people we meet in these stories live in a state of peace. They are generous, curious and welcoming, and we can happily interact with them through the magic of our travelers' stories. These stories provide little oases in a crowded and fast-paced world. For us co-editors, they re-awaken urges to travel every time we read them.

We not only get the thrill of living vicariously through someone else's travels—enjoying fond memories if we have traveled, and getting inspired if we haven't—but we also learn, through the hindsight these travelers provide, wisdom about what to do and what not to do when we actually get there. The stories serve as tantalizing tastes of what awaits us, as escapes from our daily lives.

In "Becoming History," Shannalee T'Koy writes that at one time in her life, she thought her world was the only world, but travel to distant places has changed that. "Finding myself in the minority in a sea of human beings who speak languages foreign to me, who live in a million ways differently from me, lives completely unconnected to mine, I no longer feel so important or big. But maybe by connecting myself to timeless places like Rome, and joining the invisible register of visitors who have stood where I stand, I enlarge myself. Maybe by being part of a massive whole, I'm not so insignificant after all, and as my perspective grows, so does my world."

That is the gift we offer in this new collection. Enjoy.

Martin Westerman
www.europebackpack.com

CARTOLINA POSTALE

LE PIÙ BELLE TERME DEL MONDO
SALSOMAGGIORE
PERIODO DI CURA
MARZO — NOVEMBRE

Rome was a poem
pressed into service
as a city.
- Anatole Broyard

Roma

Vatican City

The Day I Shut Down the Vatican

mary jo marcellus wyse

there they were: angels and saints everywhere; blue swirling skies mingled with blush-colored clouds; and Christ's journey to the cross. This was the culmination of my four-week excursion—countless lines, hikes through town and swelteringly hot train rides had finally led here, to Michelangelo's Sistine Chapel. It was the most heavenly place in Europe.

The quiet whisperings of tourists created a soothing white noise as I took a slow 360-degree turn, absorbing the serenity, feeling the presence of God.

"The next group will be allowed in now. All others are asked to leave," a voice boomed over the P.A. in

English, and then Italian, French and Japanese. A thin, smallish guard shooed my friends and me toward the side door with all the "others."

"Very efficient, these Vatican officials," Jami whispered. We emerged outside, blinking in the sunlight. We gazed across the grassy lawns and marble buildings of Vatican City. Then we saw the Vatican Poste. "Special Vatican stamps," I said, aware of the cheap souvenir possibilities.

Meg unzipped a pouch in her shorts. "Get me four?" she said, handing me money before she, Jami and Jake zigzagged through the crowd to a souvenir stand. I reached inside my brown leather fanny pack for my own cash and got in line at the post office. Despite its length, the line moved quickly to the counter window.

When my turn arrived, the postal clerk spoke in smooth, liquid Italian. I spoke American.

"This money. Is for. Six stamps. And this money," I said, revealing Meg's coins in my left hand, "is for. Four stamps. Separate." The man shook his head and wrinkled his brow. "OK," I said. "Six stamps ... " While I tried to explain the separate orders to him again, I noticed, out of the corner of my eye, a little boy slinking around the counter. No way was he going to jump this line. I turned my hips slightly away from him, intent on the confused brown eyes of the clerk.

Separating the coins on the counter in front of me, I began again. "This money ... " It took a few minutes before his brow finally smoothed and a smile broke on his face. "Ah, *sì!*" he said, and he proudly produced the stamps in two separate clumps. Gushing in his native tongue, he pushed them and my change through the slot in the window. I cupped my hand on the side of the ledge, slid the money into my palm, and reached for my wallet in my fanny pack. But the pack was gaping open. And my wallet was missing.

I spun around. The boy! Where had he gone? My throat tightened. I had clutched my fanny pack throughout our entire tour of Italy, in train stations, on street corners warding off Gypsy children. But on the Vatican's grounds—one place I thought would be safe—I had let down my guard.

"My wallet was stolen!" I screamed. "Did anybody see a little boy run out of here? My wallet was stolen!" The postal clerk immediately abandoned his window and hollered in Italian, initiating a few moments of panic in the Poste. Men and women spoke hastily in their own languages, creating a low-pitched murmur in the crowd. A Vatican police officer soon appeared at my side.

I was trembling, limbs twitching, my body shutting down. For one of the few moments in my life, I felt out of control. Hot tears came to my eyes. More than the loss of money, the feeling of being robbed caught off guard, hit me like an insult. Why would someone do this to me?

"It was a young boy with a yellow shirt and shorts down to here," called an American voice above the noise. I turned to see a man back in the line cut below his knees with one hand.

When the officer understood the gesture, he pinched his walkie-talkie and spilled Italian words into it. Then he flew like a pigeon from the Poste. A few feet away, a finely suited gentleman peered out the window. "What's happening?" I begged him.

He turned to face me. In an authoritatively deep voice—loud enough for the tiny room of onlookers to hear—he said, "They've closed off all Vatican exits."

An eerie silence swept across the room. Then, whispering. Translations. I heard the murmuring over and over: They've shut down the Vatican, shut down the Vatican, shut down the Vatican.

I pictured the gates coming down, armed officers planted in front of doors, hands on their machine guns. I saw families blocked in clumps asking, "Why can't we leave?" and a guard replying, "No one can. We have sealed all exits." My imaginary visitors would scratch their heads, wondering what catastrophe could have caused such an event.

In the Poste, a little gray-haired woman writing a postcard stared up at me. In a plain American accent, she said, "Don't worry. You'll get it back." She bent back over the table and continued writing. I wondered how she knew. Does this happen all the time? But I didn't speak. I couldn't. I just nodded and thought, I hope you're right, lady. I'm broke without it.

The door swung open and in rushed the police

officer. He lifted his finger, curling it inward. I followed. Outside, Jake flipped through postcards while Jami and Meg stood in line at a food stand. Seeing me with the Vatican official, they froze and stared.

"I'll be back!" I waved as I passed them, keeping up with the long legs of the officer. To my surprise, tourists paid us little attention as we charged down the sidewalk. However, when two blue-uniformed guards appeared on either side of me, I gained a few looks. Ducking under yellow ropes, and then weaving through a procession of nuns, we finally reached another corridor that led to the public Vatican restrooms.

A young boy slouched against a wall. My pace instantly slowed. But not my heart rate.

> I realized I had no idea what to look for. My gut, however, said it had to be him. How many young boys tour the Vatican alone?

"Is this him?" someone asked me.

I shook my head. I didn't know. I realized I had no idea what to look for. I remembered a boy. Small. Dark hair. Nothing else. My gut, however, said it had to be him. How many young boys tour the Vatican alone?

The guard by the bathrooms sounded like a skipping CD: "It's important for someone to identify the thief. Very important!"

"The kid wore a yellow shirt. A man at the Poste told me that." A guard took off to find the American.

Shoving his hands deep into his pockets, the

boy looked through me. I approached him. I felt like grabbing his thin, bony arms and shaking him: *Look at me! What did I ever do to you?* He wouldn't meet my eyes. A regular punk: bleached-blond hair, a deep tan, the early signs of a mustache, long shorts and scruffy sneakers.

But he wore a black shirt.

"Did you do this?" I said aloud. "Did you steal from me?" I hoped he didn't hear the tremor in my voice, see the tears rising again in my eyes. Even cornered, without an ally, without a mother to say, "Leave my son alone," he seemed incredibly calm. Even if he didn't comprehend my words, there was no mistaking my meaning. But no reaction. Not even an uncomfortable budge.

"No. Don't do that," a guard waved me off. Then a young, thin, eager guard emerged from the men's bathroom, holding a dripping-wet object at arm's length between two fingers.

"Is this it?" he asked me in impeccable English.

My breath caught. "Yes," I said. "This is mine." I held out my hand to take it. The toilet water, which weighed it down, dripped between my fingers.

I pulled out my credit card, license, student ID, blurry receipts, the mini screwdriver for my glasses and a saturated bag of Tylenol, spread the menagerie on a bench nearby, and sat down to look at it. Only my two-hundred dollars was missing.

The sound of footsteps on the marble floor caught

my attention. It was the American man and his escorts. He pointed at the boy as soon as he saw him and said, "That's him. Only without the yellow shirt. He must've taken it off and stuffed it in a garbage can."

Italian words swirled around me. The kid shrugged and shifted, shaking his head. I felt the tremors of anger return. I wanted him cuffed. A pair of officers grabbed him by the collar and lifted him into a tiny nearby room. They drew a drape so I couldn't see, but I could hear the men's loud voices and picture them poking the boy's chest until he fell backward.

Then a guard appeared, waving me to him. Plucking my recovered wet items from the bench and loading them into my fanny pack, I stood up and walked into the little room.

The boy was scowling at the ground. Happy to see a change in his countenance, I felt a sweep of satisfaction pass over me. The chief officer, in his immaculate white uniform, held all my lire and dollars in his hands. He returned the wad of bills to me and I counted. Over $200. I had made a profit! Apparently, we had a seasoned criminal on our hands. I wondered who the other victims were and whether they even knew their money was gone.

I gave the extra bills to the officer. But something else was missing. The Italian phone card I had bought at a cigarette shop in Florence. I explained this to the officials and before I knew it, the boy produced two phone cards and gave them both to me. Again a profit.

Tempted, I thought it'd be some compensation for my troubles. But, with two feet in the Vatican, I returned the second card to the policeman.

The police then whisked me, the American eye-witness and the kid to a private building in Vatican City. While the boy got an earful behind closed doors, Patrick and I signed statements, waited until papers were filed, and were released. Patrick, a man not much older than me, said he was on his honeymoon. We wished each other well. He ran off to find his wife, and I wandered back to the Poste to find my friends.

They were right where I left them—except now they all held runny ice-cream cones in sticky hands. I recounted my adventure as they licked melting streams of gelato. When I finished and the cones were all gone, Jake insisted on taking my picture in front of the Poste, to remember this day. "You know," he mused, focusing the lens, "it's probably not good PR if someone gets robbed in the Vatican. Those guards knew what was on the line."

Then Meg grinned. "How many people can send a postcard and say, 'Robbed at the Vatican. Wish you were here'?"

"You shut down the Vatican, Mary Jo," Jami said. "Put that on your postcard."

"Say 'Michelangelo!'" Jake said, and I smirked for the camera.

The shutter clicked. In the picture, I look terrified, clutching my fanny pack. Now, however, the incident makes me laugh. I got robbed. And I got everything back. Where else in Italy could that happen but the Vatican?

MARY JO MARCELLUS WYSE *admits that if she were a bit more fashion conscious, she would not have worn the problematic fanny pack in the first place. Mary Jo would like to add that she has never before or since worn a fanny pack. She recently moved to Fairbanks, Alaska, where she carries a stylish pink Nine West purse. Though it would be easier for a criminal to snag, she's not too worried. She never carries more than 10 bucks these days.*

Vatican City

Sneaking Into St. Peter's

adam emerson pachter

the Eternal City stretched out in front of us in the morning light as my friend Andrew and I arrived on the overnight train from Venice. As we looked at the vast number of sites on our map, we remembered that old saying: Rome wasn't built in a day. Even so, we were going to see it in one.

We were in the midst of a three-week backpacking tour through Europe, a high-school graduation present sponsored by our parents. Careening through northern Italy, we had spent a couple of days admiring Venice, and had been on our way to Florence, when I said that it would be a real shame to get this far and not detour to

Rome. We planned to meet another friend in the south of France in a few days, which left us only one brief opening, a single free day that we could use in between Venice and Florence. Armed with Eurail passes and a goatskin full of cheap wine, we decided to take the overnight train to Rome, wander around, and then reboard that night for the trip to Florence.

The ride down had been slightly uncomfortable. We couldn't afford a proper sleeper car, so we made do with semi-fold-down seats that didn't quite meet in the middle of the compartment, leaving a foot-wide gap that our sleeping bodies had to bridge. Generous infusions of wine made that bearable, but they didn't prepare us for the 2 a.m. awakening a conductor had in store. Opening the compartment door as we pulled into a station, he started shouting at us in Italian, and then said something that sounded like, "*Ay-oh, ay-oh, phht-phht!*" while clapping his hands and pointing down the hallway. Panicked that we were missing some necessary train connection, we gathered our stuff and ran out onto the platform.

But it was empty, deserted except for the occasional glow from a street lamp. When we finally found a porter and asked him for the train to Rome, he looked perplexed and pointed back at the car we had just left. We reboarded the train in confusion, only to find the conductor comfortably ensconced in our old compartment, feet up, enjoying a smoke. He had locked the door, so we spent the rest of the night trying to find other horizontal accommodations and grimly plotting his demise. We never saw him again, and when the train pulled into Rome, adrenaline took over, momentarily compensating for our hangovers and general fatigue.

It was a blazing hot day, and Rome in the summer really knows how to blaze. We dressed in shorts, stowed our backpacks at the luggage counter, and set out across the city. Knowing we had to be back at the station by 5 p.m., we kept a brisk pace, walking through a number of nearby churches before making our way to more famous sites like the Spanish Steps, the Colosseum and the Roman Forum. In between, we tried not to get run over by the mopeds scooting everywhere, a task complicated by the fact that lack of sleep had dulled our reflexes. Eventually, we stopped for lunch under a sun umbrella at a quiet café, and I could see that the heat had taken a toll on my friend. After devouring a sandwich, he issued his ultimatum.

"No mas," Andrew said. "I've had enough. It's just too hot to walk anymore."

"But we haven't seen the Vatican. You can't come all this way and miss St. Peter's."

"Sure I can. You go on if you want, and I'll meet you back here. While you're walking across half the city, I'll be sipping a cold beer."

While that thought was tempting, I decided I would feel foolish going to Rome and skipping the Vatican. So I took off with map in hand, marching along the road to St. Peter's. The road did seem endless after a while, and the temperature continued to climb as I crossed the Tiber River. But when I arrived, the view made up for it all: an enormous central square encircled by statues, with the grand basilica beckoning me on. I raced up the steps of the church, noticing in passing that there seemed to be a lot of people sitting on the steps in clumps and bunches, most of them looking upset. But it didn't matter to me. I had reached St. Peter's, and I was going to make Andrew wish he hadn't skipped this trip.

I was going to make Andrew wish he hadn't skipped this trip.

Preoccupied with my thoughts, I nearly ran into a guard at the entrance to the church. I stepped to the side but he followed me, holding out his arm and repeating that one Italian word that can mean almost anything: *"Prego."*

"Scusi?" I said.

"Prego," he repeated, and pointed at my legs. And then I got it. Virtually all Italian churches have a no shorts/no bare shoulders policy. Enforcement varies, but here at St. Peter's they meant business. Burdened by the heat, I had dressed in shorts without thinking through the consequences. And now they wouldn't let me in.

I tried to plead my case in English, but the guard didn't speak any. *"Prego,"* he said. I looked for a way around him, but the other guards were busy turning away other tourists with their own clothing lapses. And so I, too, sat down on the steps to the church, for the first time noticing that every other dejected-looking person on the steps also was showing too much skin for the Vatican. All these days and all these miles, and all for nothing.

There were no nearby stores selling long pants, and even I wasn't up to the challenge of trudging all the way back to the train station for a change of clothes. Besides, there wasn't enough time for that before the 5 p.m. train we had to catch. So I got up and began the long walk back to the café where I'd left Andrew. And then I suddenly received the sharpest mental image of my life, a picture as clear and distinct as if it had been painted on the air in front of me. The picture was of Andrew's face as I told him how far I'd gone, only to be turned back at the entrance to St. Peter's. I could see Andrew pause and take a sip of some refreshing beverage, nice and chilled, under the sun umbrella. And then I could see his mouth open as he laughed and laughed.

No, that couldn't be allowed to happen. One way or another, I was going to get in.

As I looked at the guards, I realized the folly of any frontal assault. There were too many of them, and I couldn't just slip through. So I started to walk around the building, hoping for some sort of side entrance. I didn't find any. But I did notice one interesting thing. The area covered by the guards was a sort of preliminary entryway. Once you passed their station, you crossed an open foyer and then went up a few steps, through an unmanned door, into the church proper. I was now standing to one side of this entrance and behind the guards, whose attention was directed entirely outward. If I could slip in this way, chances were they'd never notice. The only problem was the wrought iron fence directly in front of me.

I'd never seen such an ornate fence, and it stretched high enough that there was no chance of climbing over. Besides, that kind of maneuver would definitely catch someone's eye. I didn't see any gate, either, and when I shook the fence, nothing happened. I slumped against a nearby wall, watching other tourists pass through the guard station and into the church. So close, and yet so far. ... How was I going to get through this fence?

And then came a miraculous intervention. A member of the famous Swiss Guard, dazzling in his multicolored uniform, came up from behind, approached the fence, and began to make some adjustments with his hands. To my astonishment, an entrance suddenly appeared—a gate that the Swiss Guard opened and then closed behind him. He entered the church, never noticing me. But I had watched his movements carefully, and I went up to the fence and began to duplicate them. After a few agonizing moments, the gate re-appeared, and I slipped through it.

I then marched up the steps and into the holiest church in all of Christendom. Michelangelo's Pietà, Bernini's marble work; they all stood before me. I was so dazzled that I barely noticed the security guard waiting just inside the doors, pointing out directions to a tourist, about to turn around and notice me.

If I'd thought things through, I would have realized that of course other guards would be posted inside St. Peter's. But I didn't have time for second-guessing now. I scanned the church, desperately looking for a place to hide. A second miraculous intervention appeared. A narrow wooden corridor ran down the center of the nave, evidently so that wheelchair users wouldn't scuff St. Peter's marble floors. Two railings flanked the platform, and the wood extended solidly from the railings to the floor. I raced to the far side of the wooden corridor, pulling up behind a railing just as the guard's head swung around. The solid railing blocked his view of everything below my waist. I smiled and walked down the nave, keeping the wood between me and any guards I encountered. For the next hour, I had a magnificent tour of the most magnificent church in the world. When it was over, I walked out of the church and back through the secret gate in the side fence.

I almost danced my way back to Andrew at the café. By the time I reached him, you would have needed a yardstick to measure the smile on my face.

ADAM PACHTER *once spent an entire summer sitting in the office of Let's Go: Europe, reading dispatches by people he'd hired and sent out on the road. He vows never to repeat that mistake. Adam lives with his wife near Boston and keeps his hiking boots nearby.*

Vatican City

Don't Grope the Pope!

dave fox

every Wednesday morning, the pope holds a service for 8,000 followers at the Vatican. He rides down the aisle with the top down on his bullet-proof buggy, the popemobile. He kisses babies, blesses the crowd, and does what he can to promote peace and love. Thousands of pilgrims travel thousands of miles to hear the pontiff. A few of them freak out.

I'm not Catholic, and I realize that as an outsider, describing religious pilgrims as "freaking out" might be begging for a coach-class ticket to Hell. But please keep in mind, I was trying to help maintain the sanctity of this event.

I work as a tour guide in Scandinavia, and seeing as it was now February, there wasn't a heavy demand for my services, so I went down to Rome to stow away on a tour my friend Don was leading.

"For those of you who are interested," Don told our group, "I've arranged for an audience with Pope John Paul II." I had never had an audience with the pope before. I decided to tag along and watch respectfully from the sidelines.

I went to the Vatican expecting a solemn affair. It felt more like a rowdy World Cup soccer game. Mexican and Russian delegations held up national flags as they waited for His Holiness. Other groups waved matching colored scarves. The Americans were the most boisterous. A group of about 200 college students chanted and clapped in unison as they unfurled a large, spray-painted banner. "John Paul Two, we love you!" they cried, hoping, like groupies at a rock concert, to lure the pope onto the stage at the Vatican's indoor auditorium.

I wondered what the scene must look like in summer, when the same service would take place out in Saint Peter's Square. The Roman sun would blaze down on the crowd, causing those who had forgotten sunscreen to turn the color of lobsters.

Today's papal audience would take place inside a sprawling hall that was filled to capacity. I was five feet from the center aisle, where one of the world's most influential people would walk by in mere moments. I wanted one good photo. As the time grew closer, people began shoving: pope hooligans.

Everyone was standing on chairs now—everyone but the young nun beside me. She looked bewildered. A Puerto Rican couple tried to squeeze past a woman in my tour group, but my fellow tour member wouldn't let them through. "I've been waiting 45 minutes," she insisted. "This is my spot." A barrage of Spanish insults poured from the Puerto Ricans, along with one word in English: "knife." I was busy protecting my own vantage point. There was a shove from behind, and as I stumbled off my chair, I watched another man's video camera crash down. I had seen tamer crowds at Pearl Jam concerts.

I had seen tamer crowds at Pearl Jam concerts. Finally, the pope entered.

Finally, the pope entered. Everyone gasped. Just as I snapped my photo, a rugby match broke out in which the guy behind me attempted to get closer to God by flinging himself over the crowd to fondle the pope's robe. I ended up with a photo of the man's back.

My new digital camera was taking an eternity to cycle for another picture. Then, just as it warmed up, the pope moved, perfectly centered, into my viewfinder. It would be the photo of a lifetime. I pressed the button. The red-eye light flashed. My camera beeped feebly. And just as the shutter clicked, up went the hand of the woman beside me, right in front of my lens. I took a perfectly centered picture of her camera.

Twenty seconds later, the pope was far away, continuing his journey to the stage. I had just seen him up close, only it was through my camera lens—like seeing him on TV. Now he was a vague white blur off in the distance. I had a photo to prove how close I was, but I felt like I hadn't seen him at all.

On our way out, after the English part of the service, the woman who had claimed to be wielding a knife was waiting for us. She stepped in our way, waving her fist. "Let's go outside," she said menacingly to the woman she had jostled with earlier.

"You want to fight ... *in the Vatican?!*" I asked.

"She pushed me!" she sputtered. "You want to fight? I like to fight!"

Well, I don't like to fight. Especially in the presence of prominent world religious leaders. Instead, I seized the opportunity to feed my ego. For days, I had been an off-duty tour guide. Don was the one in charge, and I was the lost tourist. I was used to being in the spotlight, commanding the tour group's attention. Don wasn't with us right now. This was my chance to be a hero. I spoke French. I could explain to the Swiss soldiers who guard the Vatican what was going on.

It's difficult to ask a Vatican guard to protect you, though. Their main weapon in defending Vatican City is the court-jester costumes they wear. If anybody tries to attack, the guard moves into the attacker's way, causing him or her to fall down in a convulsive fit of laughter at unquestionably the world's silliest military uniforms.

I tried to keep a straight face, but I had another problem. I had skipped French class the day the teacher taught us how to say, "This woman is a psychotic freak who is threatening to stab us in the presence of the pope."

After several botched attempts, I constructed a halfway grammatical sentence. "This woman is being very violent. She is attacking us." The guard looked at me like I was the insane one. Our assailant smirked calmly in the distance. Desperate, I switched to English. "She's following us," I said. "She's crazy. Will you please make sure she doesn't follow us outside?"

He didn't understand me. I was begging this man to protect us, but he wasn't getting it. And the only thing he really looked capable of doing was juggling and playing the lute.

The woman followed us outside. I don't know for how long she stalked us. We ignored her and she eventually went away. Perhaps the Vatican guards figured out what was up and stopped her. Perhaps it finally dawned on her that slugging somebody in front of the pope might cost her a few points in the afterlife.

Mob psychology makes people do crazy things. It's why there's football violence in England. It's why people get trampled at rock concerts. I had thought that at a papal audience, of all places, people would respect each other. But when you put 8,000 strangers in a room together for any reason, something far more powerful than sanity or spirituality takes over.

DAVE FOX *is a freelance humor and travel writer, a public speaker, and a Rick Steves tour guide. In 2004, he won the Erma Bombeck Writers' Workshop Book Proposal Contest for his book of travel humor essays, "Getting Lost: Mishaps of an Accidental Nomad." This story is excerpted from that book. He teaches classes on how to write more vivid travel journals (www.traveljournaling.com) and is writing a book on the same topic. You can find him at www.davesbook.com.*

Rome

Becoming History

shannalee t'koy

On a warm March afternoon, when my American friends and family were just sitting down to breakfast, when people in Moscow were just eating dinner, and people in Beijing were sound asleep, I saw it. The dense crowd of tourists around it, pushing and elbowing, filling the air with their clamorous cacophony of voices, remained contentedly oblivious. Using it to frame and snap friend-filled photographs, glancing upon it for fractions of seconds before resuming conversations and dancing onward, they seemed barely aware.

But I, who had been occupied with sifting through silk ties and inventorying my souvenir purchases, looked up and suddenly stood awestruck, in the presence of a monumental creation worlds larger than myself.

I was standing in a little shop. Moments before, I had been walking in Rome, where I had been inhaling history and absorbing sights into my mental scrapbook, joining photographs together in my mind. I knew that millions of people had come to this location before me, and millions would come after. But for me, that day, at that moment, I stood in the presence of magnificence, and my feet rooted me to the cobblestones. It was like a dream, and I kept telling myself, *I'm in Italy*, as if the dramatic surroundings couldn't fully convince me. I hoped that in that moment, I could make it mine, possess it, so that it would belong to me from then on.

It was Trevi Fountain. The cloudless indigo backdrop of the sky threw its every detail into radiant, sunkissed relief. Most awesome was its size: everything about its massive pillars and sculpture dwarfed the people at its base. I had seen this work of art miniaturized in postcards and on television screens, but I could see now that they did the real thing an injustice. This Trevi Fountain took my breath away. I was forced to step back to behold its entirety.

The central statue, of the legendary Roman sea-god Neptune, seemed supernatural above the horses half-immersed in frothing water beneath him. Omniscient and powerful, the mythological god rose highest in the fountain, riding his shell-like chariot with his gaze fixed on the square around him, as if he controlled its movements. Surrounded by tall orange and yellow buildings, his majesty's appearance was fantastic in the bustling square, and he invited us to believe there was magic in the fountain's splashing turquoise pool.

A steady stream of people flowed around the fountain's edges. Tourists followed Roman legend by tossing wish-filled coins into the water. If the thousands of coins covering the fountain's floor were any indication, countless travelers had trusted this frozen Neptune to alter their destinies for good, and guarantee them a return to Rome. I found myself imagining centuries of these wishers, clad in different apparel, carrying different burdens than mine or my fellow travelers', but admiring this marvelous sight just like us. Through all this, the fountain stood. In that moment, I sensed that Trevi wasn't becoming part of my history; I was becoming part of its.

> **I found myself imagining centuries of these wishers.**

A child I know recently mentioned how far away we Chicago natives lived from New York. His innocence made me laugh, but I suppose, at his age, I viewed places like New York as infinitely distant, too. I thought Third World countries and war and violence couldn't be important if they were that far away. I thought of England and China as being other planets entirely, and when my dad traveled overseas, I couldn't comprehend his inhabiting a place so far away the same way he would inhabit our house on our street in America.

That was a time when I thought that my world was the only world; when I thought that the way people in my world acted was the way everyone else in the world acted. Now, my travels have landed me in a sea of human beings who speak languages foreign to me, who live differently from me in a million ways, and whose lives are completely unconnected to mine. I no longer feel so important or big. But maybe by connecting myself to timeless places like Rome, and joining the invisible register of visitors who have stood where I stand, I enlarge myself. Maybe by being part of a massive whole, I'm not so insignificant after all, and as my perspective grows, so does my world.

As I watched the crowd in front of the Trevi, a group of tourists gathered by a tall lamppost to take photographs. A few young Roman men perched atop a raised stone step, laughing about the passing characters. Two suited businessmen wandered through the crowd, immune to the surrounding noise.

People spread through the three intersecting roads that lead to the fountain. Some peered through camera lenses, moving continually backward as they tried to capture the sculpture in one frame. Some moved beyond the landmark to nearby streets, in search of gelato, watercolor paintings or souvenirs. All this, under the same perfect, deep-blue sky I have seen at home, the one that graces every country and city on Earth.

Long after we're gone, the fountain will remain, and future visitors will come, remark on its grandeur and snap photographs. And many more will throw coins loaded with wishes into its waters, to barter with destiny under Neptune's steady gaze.

SHANNALEE T'KOY *is a twenty-something graduate student living in the Chicago area. She enjoys expanding her horizons through school, travel and reading.*

Rome

Night Bus

brad o'brien

the Easy Internet Café in Rome's Piazza Barberina was my office. I was working as an online writing tutor and hoping to find a job teaching English, so that I'd never have to leave the Eternal City. Every night, I would work from 9 p.m. until the café closed at 2 a.m., then walk back to my hotel. But after a few weeks, finding neither a teaching job nor a more permanent residence, I moved my bag of clothes and books into a cheap bed and breakfast about 30 minutes by train from Piazza Barberina.

Then I remembered that the commuter trains stop running at about 9 p.m. That meant I had to skip work; spend the night in Stazione Termini, the city's main train station; or figure out the night bus routes. I liked none of these options. My online tutoring job enabled me to live as a drifter, and I didn't want to risk losing that. I wouldn't have minded sitting up all night reading and drinking coffee in the train station, but I didn't want to spend the next day sleeping.

Trains gave me no trouble. Their stations are clearly labeled, so I always knew when I'd arrived at my stop. But buses confused me. I'd board knowing which street I wanted, but unless I could read the small street sign as the bus came to it, I was apt to miss it—or else I never knew where along a street to get off the bus—so I'd usually end up in places I didn't want to go.

My aversion to buses started in Dublin. I'd spent my last night there in a pub with new friends, then caught what I thought was the last bus of the night back to my hotel. I sat next to a window watching carefully for my stop, but I missed it. I climbed off at the end of the route, in the middle of some neighborhood 45 minutes' walk from the hotel.

I'd forgotten this experience when I stepped off the plane at Marco Polo International Airport on my first visit to Italy. I assumed I'd have no problem taking a bus to my hotel in Mestre, a small industrial town next door to Venice, and that I'd be exploring the city of canals within an hour. I boarded what I thought was the right bus, and then looked out from my window seat for the train station that was across the street from my hotel. I was still looking when my bus reached the end of its route, in a parking lot opposite the entrance to the Grand Canal. Chagrined, I rode back to the airport and boarded a different bus. A few hours later, when I finally arrived at the hotel, all I wanted to do was sleep.

In Rome a week later, awake and over my jet lag, I tried catching a bus from Piazza Venezia to an area called Trastevere. With no idea where to get off, and not wanting to annoy the bus driver or anyone else by asking questions in broken Italian, I stepped off in an area that looked interesting. But it wasn't Trastevere. After wandering around hoping to stumble upon a restaurant my guidebook recommended, I gave up, caught a bus back to Rome's historic center, and resolved not to ride buses any more.

If I wanted to keep my job and still sleep at night, I realized, I had to learn to ride buses.

But if I wanted to keep my online tutoring job and still sleep at night, I realized there was no way around it: I had to learn to ride buses. So I bought the most detailed map of Rome I could find and located the night bus stops near Piazza Barberina. Matching street names on my map with the names on the signs, I traced what I thought was the route to the bed and breakfast, and identified the number of what I hoped was the right bus.

That night, I finished my tutoring session just before 2 a.m., walked down Via del Tritone and over to Via del Corso, and waited for the bus. It arrived within 10 minutes. I sat down and prepared to watch the street signs closely. Within a few minutes, the driver pulled into Piazza Venezia, parked and turned off the lights. Assuming he was simply saving energy while waiting for more passengers, I kept my seat. The buses run between two end points, making several stops along the way, and Piazza Venezia was one of these stops.

The driver told me to leave the bus. Sensing my confusion, he pointed out another bus that followed the same route. Apparently, his shift had ended, or perhaps he was simply taking a break, so I boarded the other bus and waited for its driver.

About 15 minutes later, the new driver showed up, started the engine, and pulled into the dark streets that I hoped led to my temporary home. If I hadn't been so concerned with reading the signs blurring past my window, I would have enjoyed the ride. As the bus made its way to the outskirts of Rome, it circled ancient ruins, sped past Baroque churches, crossed the Tiber and turned down atmospheric, tree-lined streets. At the end of one of these, the driver finally had to stop for a red light, enabling me to read a sign that confirmed I was on the right bus. Now I just had to figure out where to get off.

On my map, I could trace a clear path from the street I recognized to the bed and breakfast, so I considered getting off the bus and walking the rest of the way. I reached for the red button that would signal the driver to let me off, then reconsidered. The area outside my window looked scary. It was poorly lit; the newsstands, buildings and sidewalks were covered in graffiti; and I had no idea if I'd be walking for minutes or hours.

I stayed on and continued watching for Viale Medaglie d'Oro. A few minutes later, the bus turned onto this street. I started feeling like a Roman and wondering why I had been so worried about finding my way home. But this street was long. I needed to get to Piazza Giovenale. Via Marziale and Via Galimberti connected it with Viale Medaglie d'Oro, so I watched carefully for these two streets.

Soon I was the only passenger left on the bus, and the driver and I had left Viale Medaglie d'Oro far behind. It was 3 a.m. The sun would rise in a few hours, so I figured the worst that could happen was that I would ride back and forth between the route's two endpoints until it was light enough for me to feel comfortable stepping off on a street I recognized. Then I could walk the rest of the way to the bed and breakfast. The driver had a kind face, so I didn't expect him to mind.

But when he parked on a side street in a residential area, turned around and noticed I was still sitting in my seat, it was obvious that he did mind. He said something in Italian that I couldn't understand, so I made a loop with my pointer finger to indicate that I planned to ride back around. Annoyance replaced the kindness in his face. He turned to his left, looked out the open window and unleashed a mouthful of Italian—that language that sounds beautiful even when it's about something you'd probably rather not hear.

When the driver had finished telling the night how much of a pain in the ass I was, he turned back around and asked, "*Dove sta andando?*"

I answered, "*Viale Medaglie d'Oro*," and more poetic exasperation flowed from his tongue. Appearing to have given up on me, he turned the bus around and started his route back to Piazza Venezia. All I could do was sit back and wait for the sun to rise.

About 15 minutes later, the driver slowed down, looked back at me and indicated that he was turning onto Viale Medaglie d'Oro. He seemed to be asking where on this street I needed to go, so I moved to the seat closest to him and showed him my map. He pulled over, turned on the light, took the map in his hands and studied it closely.

With only kindness in his face, he drove slowly down the street looking for Via Galimberti. Each time he approached a side street, he stopped to read its sign, and his patience never wavered.

He finally stopped to pick up a passenger, and as the man stepped on board, the driver asked if he knew whether Via Galimberti was nearby. It was, and the passenger pointed it out to us. "*Grazie*" seemed such an inadequate expression for the gratitude I felt for the driver, but it was all I knew to say as I stepped off the bus.

During my short walk to the bed and breakfast, I wondered whether the driver had really been annoyed with me, or if it had simply seemed this way because his language sounds much more expressive than mine. It didn't matter. By the time I got off the bus, he'd given me yet another example of the Italian friendliness that always amazes me.

The following night, I left the Easy Internet Café confident I would make it back to the bed and breakfast long before sunrise. This time, I knew exactly where to go.

BRAD O'BRIEN *didn't find a job in Rome, but by the time he left, he was helping other Americans figure out the bus routes. He has a B.A. and an M.A. in English from the University of South Carolina. Before deciding that the settled life wasn't for him, he taught composition for three years at Francis Marion University. He lives in Myrtle Beach, South Carolina, teaching English and planning his next overseas adventure.*

Rome

Lost in Transit

gloria fallon

geneva had been a disaster, and the six of us couldn't wait to get to Italy. A violent windstorm in Switzerland's peaceful capital had blown away our plans for sightseeing: The river cruise was canceled, the Jet d'Eau fountain was shut down, and we were nearly flung from the top of a cathedral tower by what seemed to be a Category Four gust of wind.

So Italy looked golden and promising to the south, offering all the sightseeing a tourist could dream of in Rome, and gondola rides galore in Venice.

We came early to the Geneva train station, but when our train to Rome finally arrived, we couldn't find our car. Under the enormous weight of our rucksacks, the six of us frantically began lumbering down the platform in search of Car 311. This ludicrous sight probably would have made me laugh if overnight trains to Rome had left Geneva every 15 minutes instead of once a day. We couldn't afford to miss this train. When our search finally proved futile, I yelled, "Just get on!" and we scrambled into the nearest car. Well, me, Patty, Eileen and Stephanie did.

"Where're Deb and Rachel?" Stephanie panted. As Eileen and I briefly cast obligatory looks around, certain that our friends had made the train, Patty slung off her rucksack and hopped back onto the platform to look for them. And with no warning, no "All aboard!," no call to action that we typical English-speaking-only Americans could comprehend, the train doors shut. And the train started moving. Were only three of us on our way to Rome now?

And with no warning, no "All aboard!," the train doors shut. And the train started moving.

Hunched and wild-eyed under my rucksack, I went barging down the narrow corridor and threw open the doors to the adjoining car. There were Deb and Rachel, but no sign of Patty. She had been left on the platform.

I started to panic. Not since our bacchanalian weekend in Amsterdam had I felt so sick. Could we stop the train? How would Patty get to Rome by herself? What would I do if I were left behind in a country where no one spoke English?

We regrouped in our crowded compartment and tried to put ourselves in Patty's shoes. As her closest friend in the bunch, I knew that she carried her passport in the money holder she wore around her neck, so we were comforted knowing she at least had that. We got out our Eurail timetables and figured that, to make her way to Rome, she'd have to board a train that stopped in Milan. After some quick deliberation, we decided that Stephanie and Deb, with their faltering command of French (the best we could do), would go to Milan to meet the train we all hoped Patty would take. Satisfied that we had successfully planned her journey and arrival time at Roma Termini, we started to arrange our couchette for the night ahead.

As the designated keeper of Patty's abandoned rucksack, I had to dig through her bag to find the alarm clock we all depended on. In our little group, each of us played a certain role, and Patty's absence was noticeable. She was our cheerful traveler, the one we lovingly called "Pollyanna Patty." She was happy to sightsee through rain and wind, and willing to share whatever she had when one of us was in need.

It was heartbreaking to rummage past the canary-yellow jacket she brought so she wouldn't get lost in a crowd, and I sadly held up her favorite Yankees cap for all to see. We started sharing our favorite memories about Patty, until Eileen, the realist of the group, piped in, "She's not dead, for God's sake, just lost. We're going to see her in a few hours."

This lightened the mood a little, but we all had trouble falling asleep, not knowing where Patty was sleeping.

The next morning we awoke to the beautiful sight of the Italian countryside, with green rolling hills and sweet little cream houses topped with terracotta tile roofs. The gorgeous scenery wasn't enough to lift our spirits, though, because now our group was down to three—Stephanie and Deb had switched to the Milan train in the middle of the night. Eileen, Rachel and I pulled into Roma Termini around 9:30 a.m. and sat down at the snack bar to wait for the rest of our group to arrive.

Not an hour later, a smiling Patty emerged from the Milan train, followed by Stephanie and Deb. We were overjoyed. Our plan had worked! We were together again! We crowded around Patty, hugging and kissing her and asking her how she spent the horrible night. We couldn't have been more surprised by her response. "I had the best time! Italians are the nicest people on earth!" she exclaimed, showing us a stash of cigarettes, candy, a magazine and numerous phone numbers she had received from sympathetic travelers.

"I'm just really tired because I didn't get much sleep," she said. "I spent most of the night talking to this hot guy named Francesco. We're supposed to meet up tonight at the Trevi Fountain. Talk about romantic. Boy, do I love Italy!"

The five of us who had worried all night and all

morning looked at each other in disbelief. Now each of us wished we were the "lucky" one who had gotten lost.

GLORIA FALLON *is a travel and humor writer, and co-author of the humor book, "I Hate This Place: The Pessimist's Guide to Life." An anglophile since studying abroad in London during her junior year at Siena College in New York, Gloria frequently visits in-laws in England and France. Since their European vacation, Gloria and Patty have traveled together to Germany, Wales, Ireland and Iceland, and neither has gotten lost.*

Rome to Syracuse

Masters of the Southern Italy Night

brandy fleming

It was almost midnight when I rushed from my train through Rome's central station, looking for the train that would carry me to Syracuse, on the southeast corner of the Mediterranean's largest island, Sicily. That was my final destination, after a whirlwind weekend at Oktoberfest in Munich. *Four minutes to catch the train,* my mind buzzed. I was hungry. In the rush, I had forgotten to eat dinner.

Confusing signs. Must practice my Italian, my mind chattered as I ran past the platform for Naples. Three minutes to find my train. Last night's world-famous German brew had affected my normally clear mind.

That was a good thing in the crowded Munich festival tents, where I had jumped up on long wooden tables to dance many a jig. But it wasn't very helpful now, when I needed some good judgment to find my way through the crowded train station. *Why is this backpack so heavy? Must get sleep.*

There are risks and rewards to budget globetrotting. Even a cursory review of the safety tips online and in European guidebooks reveals that southern Italy is not the best place for a lone female to travel, let alone thread her way through the Italian capital's main train station in the middle of the night. *Where is my train? I've only got a minute left!*

I was on my seventh month of solo backpacking around the world. After swimming with whale sharks in Australia and hiking volcanic craters in New Zealand, I was making my way from Scandinavia south through central Europe. I had pretty much dumped the safety advice because, with my intuition and natural chatter, I'd found the people and places of the world to be quite friendly. Also, my budget at this point was on a financial version of the Atkins diet. So, when I purchased my ticket to Sicily, I was far more concerned about economics than safety.

My two challenges now were to make the train before it departed, and to make sure I boarded the right carriage. The 20 carriages of my train would be splitting before dawn, half continuing southward to Reggio di Calabria on the boot-shaped mainland, the other half crossing the narrow Messina Strait to Sicily. A few nights earlier, on an overnight train from Denmark to Germany, I had shared a cabin with a Brazilian lad who'd stored his backpack in a separate carriage. He awoke in the morning to the startling news that, while he had arrived safe and sound in Munich, his pack had split in the middle of the night for Frankfurt. I had to be careful, or I'd end up at the wrong destination, too.

The upside of backpacking is that all of life's necessary material possessions fit with liberating simplicity into one bag. The downside is that such simplicity can disappear at once if that bag is lost or stolen.

Relief! There was the carriage. I could feel my breath and pulse slow as I chose a six-seat compartment, already occupied by an elderly Italian man. He looked worn, and I wondered what life events had peppered his hair gray and deepened the laugh lines around his dark eyes. As I heaved my pack into the overhead luggage rack, a younger Italian joined us. He looked to be about my age, and he spoke just a little English. The men exchanged greetings, and the younger turned to me and asked if I could speak Italian: *"Parla Italiano?"* I responded apologetically, *"No, sono Americano."*

If we had boarded a day train, we would have been able to see the Italian countryside passing outside our windows, dotted with sunflowers and vineyards—one of the finer treasures in a budget traveler's trek across Europe. Instead, the bulk of my 10-hour ride would offer occasional glimpses of deserted, dimly lighted village train stations. I decided to pass the first few hours practicing my recently acquired knitting skills. My fellow travelers looked interested, so, using family photos, my dog-eared Italian-English dictionary, and several rounds of charade moves, I finally managed to convey to them that I was knitting a scarf for my young nephew back home. They smiled acknowledgement and continued chatting as they watched me knit row after row.

When a tall, uniformed Trenitalia attendant leaned in the doorway to punch our tickets, he exchanged a few words with the men, and they all laughed heartily. *Learn to speak Italian, pronto,* I chided myself. The attendant nodded toward me, and then made a motion across the door as if to indicate that the men should close it. This aroused my curiosity. What were these men talking about, and what did the gesture mean?

As I stowed my knitting and stretched my legs out into the seat in front of me, I patted myself on the back for choosing the window seat. I planned to catch a few hours of sleep before we crossed over to Sicily in the morning, and I looked forward to the sea scenery once daylight returned.

The older Italian slid the compartment door closed and drew the curtains tightly. He rose and pulled down his faded black duffel bag from the overhead luggage rack. *That's strange,* I thought, uneasily watching him rummage through the sack. I expected him to pull out a travel pillow, perhaps a toothbrush to freshen up, or maybe an alarm clock to make sure he didn't miss his stop during the night.

But what emerged from his worn bag were heavy-duty ropes, rubber bungee straps, and long lengths of welded steel chain. My curious composure turned into alarm, then panic, as each link of chain spilled out and he and the younger Italian turned toward me. The collection looked like a homemade bondage kit, and now I was trapped in the corner by the window. Escape was futile, and my screams never would be heard over the rattle of the train speeding along the tracks.

That's strange,
I thought,
uneasily
watching
him rummage
through the sack.

They both began gesturing at me while the younger guy attempted in broken English to convey their intent. *"Night. You. Bad. Train. Man. Bad. OK? OK."* I was thinking, *NO! This is NOT OK! What is going on?!* The older man waved his arms adamantly across the door, trying to show me what he would accomplish with his assortment of shackling apparatus.

On the brink of tears, I somehow managed to summon my mental clarity; it finally clicked that the pair were not going to chain me to the luggage rack. Had I checked with any seasoned backpacker before boarding the train, I would have learned that robbery and assault are common problems on overnight, intercity trains in southern Italy. It is highly recommended that women do not travel alone on these trips. My adrenaline level dropped and my pulse slowed as I watched the elder Italian work with stealth at securing the door. Intricately wound over and under each other, the ropes, cords and chains looked like a Harry Houdini creation that even the Incredible Hulk would be hard-pressed to break through. My compartment companions made themselves comfortable and soon were snoozing soundly. With one eye open, I pretended to sleep, now wary about what lurked outside the cabin door, and not certain that this pair of sleeping beauties could be trusted.

The elderly Italian stirred around 5 a.m. and began collecting his belongings. As the train slowed for the next stop, he unwound the security contraption from the door and returned the shackling kit to his bag. With a nod of his head and a warm *arrivederci*, my protective Houdini stole away into the early-morning darkness.

Now it was just the two of us, me and the younger Italian, alone in the compartment. Unable to put off Mother Nature's calling any longer, I left him behind in apparent slumber as I set out to find the restroom. After glancing into the third of several compartments down the narrow corridor, I realized that I was indeed the only female in the carriage. The uneasy feeling returned to the pit of my stomach as I realized that several of the men were awake, and watching me. I hurried to the restroom and locked the door with the earnest intention of remaining there until my daddy came to rescue me, or until the train arrived in Syracuse, whichever happened first.

I splashed water on my face, summoned my fleeting wits, and remembered that I had left my backpack behind in the unsecured compartment. As the train slowed again for the next stop, I reluctantly unbolted the door and forced myself out into the shadowy darkness, tiptoeing back down the hall, hoping to go unnoticed.

The young Italian, looking like an innocent Casanova, shifted slightly in his slumber as I crawled back over to the consolation of my window seat. I pretended to sleep, calculating the minutes left until sunrise, wanting this train ride to be over. Just as I was starting to settle down, something brushed slowly across my leg. I jumped, my pulse throbbing in my throat now, my mind racing once again. The brush turned into a stroke as Casanova's hand crept up the lower half of my leg. I bolted upright and jerked my leg away.

Casanova casually leaned forward, blocking the only escape route. I could see the intense desire in his mischievous eyes, the amorous look that Italian males are famous for. In a low, seductive tone, he suddenly spoke smooth, fluent English, free of any grammatical clumsiness. *"Brandy, do you like the stars? Can you see the light of the moon? Your eyes, they are beautiful. Where are you going in Sicily? Do you have a boyfriend?"*

I replied that yes, indeed, I did have a very big, mean, jealous and slightly psychotic boyfriend—as if all of those attributes were going to magically rescue me now. Casanova continued his wooing as the train loaded into the hollow belly of the Messina Strait ferry. Everything went pitch black. *Great,* I thought, curling my legs up against me in the seat, as far away as possible from Casanova's hands. I longed to be back in Munich, carefree again, dancing on the tables at *Oktoberfest.* I considered leaving to find another compartment, but it was so creepy in the corridor, I felt more confident resisting my Casanova's insistent infatuation than facing whatever unknowns lurked outside.

He persisted at trying to persuade me to get off the train with him in Messina. *"I have apartment in good part of town. You stay with me. I be tour guide for you."* I groped under the seat for my knitting needles, confident I could pull off some sophisticated martial-arts move with the long, pointed metal. But now he was keeping his hands to himself, so I let him rattle on as I mentally hurried the ferry across the water.

After what seemed like eons, the ferry docked at Syracuse, and the hold finally opened to release the train. The sky reappeared outside my window, the twinkle of fading stars giving way to the approaching sunrise. The hills behind the city were speckled with the lights of households and bakeries waking to greet the early morning. The train rolled slowly on the tracks toward its stop in the city. Casanova gathered his belongings and attempted to charm me with one last wink. Then he was gone.

Innocence returned to my world. Heaving the compartment door closed and pulling the curtains tight, I felt flooded with relief. The welcome daylight made the past night's events fade away like the waves receding into the sea alongside our train. Houdini and Casanova had given me a new understanding of Italian culture—and a reminder that there's a reason for those safety warnings to globetrotting backpackers.

BRANDY FLEMING *is a freelance writer and seasoned nomad who claims a base camp in North Carolina. She traded her corporate job and business suits for this yearlong backpacking trek. She explores the globe in pursuit of her lifelong dream to experience every state in the country and every country in the world.*

Vatican City

Guidebook as Gospel

campbell jefferys

The line stretched along Viale Vaticano and around the corner down Via Leone. I couldn't even see the entrance of the Vatican Museum when I joined the end of the queue. It was only by asking the man in front of me that I confirmed I was in line for it. That was how the conversation started.

"The guidebook says the line moves quickly," the man said, with a nonchalant smile. He seemed young, but the dashes of gray in his hair and through his stubble made him look older. His small daypack was full, with a metal canister wedged into a side pocket. When he turned around to talk to me, his rain jacket lifted, and I saw the black band of the money belt he wore.

"Guidebooks?" said another man, his young face smooth with just enough puppy fat to make you want to give his cheeks a good squeeze. "Don't believe a word that's in them."

The first man had been clutching an Italy guidebook in his gloved hand. He opened it and held it like he was reading from the Bible. Defiantly, he read aloud that visitors to the Vatican Museum should not be put off by a long queue because it actually moves quite quickly.

"Most people are heading straight for the Sistine Chapel," he read, snapping the book shut and perhaps restraining himself from saying, "Here endeth the lesson." A ripple of movement ran through the crowd and we shuffled forward. The man smiled, as if this quick advancement proved his point.

"He's right," said a young woman standing behind me. I turned to look at her and was surprised to see that the line had grown considerably since I had joined; mostly young backpackers, a few seniors. "But this is nothing," she continued. "You should see the lines in the summer. They start almost at St Peter's."

It was a cool December morning, brisk and windy but bright. The sunshine made the buildings of Rome glow, a fitting scene of religiosity.

"Still, I wouldn't go anywhere with one of them books," said the second man. He slammed a Mets baseball cap onto his head and zipped his fleece up to his chin. We were out of the sun now, the high wall of the Vatican City casting us in shadow. "They poison your trip, if you know what I mean; take all the fun out of traveling."

The first man opened his mouth to answer, but a friend of the girl jumped in.

"That's rubbish," she said. She dug around in her daypack and took out her own guidebook, a Europe compilation. "I never would've survived this trip if not for this book. You don't have to live by it, but it sure makes things a lot easier."

"Absolutely," the first girl said. "I was in Cambodia last year, and you can't travel there without a guidebook, especially if you're a woman."

"Okay," the second man conceded. He seemed to like the look of the first girl and even stepped out of his place in line to continue the conversation standing next to her. The girls exchanged a glance at this move. "Guidebooks have their merits. But I've done my whole Europe trip without a book." He pointed his finger at the girl's Europe guide. "I mean, look at the size of that thing. It's as heavy as a telephone book."

"That's because it's full of information," I said, a smile creeping across my face.

"But not all of it's necessary," mused the first man. "When I did my first backpacking trip, I actually ripped out all the chapters I didn't think were necessary. Cut the book in half."

The line moved forward and we were carried along, but the conversation continued in earnest. Should I tell them now or wait until the end?

"I like reading about history," said the second girl. "And I like the reviews of hostels and restaurants."

"But they're just someone's opinion," another man responded, his voice revealing the trace of an accent. He was tall, and he stood behind the two girls almost protectively, especially now that the boy in the Mets cap stood so close to the first girl. "Why should you go to a place or not based on one person's impression?"

I smiled. "That is, of course, assuming the person even went there. It could be a secondhand opinion, maybe thirdhand, or, worse, a reader's recommendation."

The boy in the Mets cap nodded his head at me, thinking I was on his side. "And the information is always out of date."

"But it does give you an idea of what to expect," said the first man. He took the metal canister from his backpack. Steam came out when he opened the top, and the strong fragrance of coffee invaded our nostrils, making us all sniff at the air with our eyes closed. "Even if the prices are slightly wrong, you've still got"—he smiled at the Mets cap—"a ballpark figure."

The two girls laughed and the boy flushed slightly, his puffy cheeks turning a splotchy pink.

"The books are always badly updated," I said.

"How would *you* know?" the first girl asked.

I opened my mouth to answer, but the tall man interjected. "It depends on which book you have."

"They're all crap," the boy muttered, his face still

slightly red. He was now a few steps in front of the girls, standing next to me, with his back to them.

"If you don't want to travel with them, you don't have to," said the second girl, stuffing her big Europe guide back into her daypack.

We shuffled forward again and were already around the corner. Over the top of the crowd, I could see the entrance to the museum.

"I think what he's trying to say is that you should experience a country on your own and not through one of these books," said the tall man.

"Well, that's true," said the graying man. "There's nothing worse than backpackers who walk around countries with their heads buried in a guidebook."

"The point of travel is to experience things for yourself," said the first girl. "The guide just helps you along the way."

"I wouldn't have seen half the things I've seen if not for my guidebook," added her friend.

Closer to the entrance, the line moved slowly and intermittently. But the lively conversation made the time pass quickly, and it distracted us from the cold.

An older woman, standing in front of the first man, turned around. Her face was lined but she carried her years well, and she held herself with a graceful confidence, a woman of the world. She smiled and looked quickly at each of our faces.

"Say what you want about those books you have," she said softly, "but one thing's for sure, they've made traveling a whole lot easier. I can't stay in a hostel anymore because they're always booked out. It's a shame. Hostels were always great places to meet people."

I frowned. Although I was still young enough to mix with the Gap Year crowd, I also was old enough and well-traveled enough to appreciate what she meant. The guidebooks had succeeded paradoxically at opening up travel to a range of people who, 10 years ago, laughed at those who went off backpacking. Where in the past you could easily journey from place to place without organizing your trip, now you had to make reservations and credit-card bookings and get reference numbers. It was hardly the world experience you had set off to have.

The guidebooks had succeeded paradoxically at opening up travel.

....

On this trip through Italy, I had found myself booking hostels in advance to be sure I would get a cheap bed, and I had lamented to anyone who would listen, like some wizened old geezer, that traveling wasn't what it used to be.

"And they're not exactly cheap anymore either," I added.

The older woman cocked an eyebrow at me. "Still cheaper than hotels, though."

"Not by much."

"Can there be a place less atmospheric than a hotel?" complained the boy in the Mets cap. "Just a bunch of suited Joes and sales-rep Marys. Where's the fun in that?"

We entered the museum and split up. The Vatican Museum is an extraordinary place. The main draw is Michelangelo's Sistine Chapel, and the tourists crowd in, straining their necks to look up at the ceiling. There's Adam reaching out his hand to God, and the image is so powerful, you can only stare at it in wonder.

"Now, how could you explain that in a guidebook?" said the boy in the Mets cap. He sidled up next to me and both of us looked up, our eyes locked on Adam's outstretched finger. "This has to be experienced."

The two girls arrived, the tall man in tow. We all smiled hello and stood in a small group, our chins pointing at the ceiling. We all let out breathless sighs.

"It's much better since they restored it," said the older woman from the queue. She had a soft smile on her face. "I was here almost twenty years ago. You couldn't really see anything. Now look at it—just as Michelangelo would have seen it."

"Does anyone know when this place closes?' asked the man with the flecks of gray. "My book says 6 p.m."

"Mine says 5:30," said one of the girls.

I laughed and rubbed my straining neck.

"Who updates these books anyway?" asked the man.

"They're all idiots," said the boy in the Mets cap. "Probably just a bunch of guys sitting at computers. Probably never traveled anywhere in their lives."

"Hey, be nice to the updaters," I said, a tad too scornfully.

"Why?" they all asked in unison.

"Because I'm one of them. And the museum closes at 4:45, which is in about half an hour. Who wants a latte? I know a great place."

BORN IN KALAMUNDA, *near Perth, Campbell first traveled in Australia before taking lengthy trips to New Zealand, Indonesia, North America and Europe. He has contributed to Rough Guide books on the U.S., Europe and Germany, and he works now as a freelance journalist. His first novel, "The Bicycle Teacher," was published last year in the U.K.*

Rome to Civitavecchia

Gelato Girls

courtney mcdermott

he train cabin was stuffy with old air and sleeping
bodies packed up next to one another, head to
toe. It was one of those cabins with two rows of seats
facing each other, which pulled out to make one big
bed. I slept near the door and my best friend, Kiska,
practically hugged my legs. "I was being molested!" she
whispered dramatically to me when we woke up that
morning. "That's why I kept getting closer to you. He
just kept rubbing up against me!"

"He" was an unkempt Italian man of indistin-
guishable age who said very little. He was sandwiched
between us and a middle-aged Italian couple who kept
whispering about us *ragazze*, us girls. I shrugged off his

behavior as Italian machismo. Hey, it will be a good story to tell, I told her.

Kiska and I had visited Italy before and were here again on a whim. She was studying in London, I in Galway, and we were meeting up for a three-week spring break, determined to have ourselves the complete "European backpack adventure."

We started in hotels in Paris, and then moved south to a fabulous hostel in Nice. But, between the rocky beaches and the rain, we couldn't enjoy the beach bathing we had planned. So, in a daring moment, we spontaneously took an overnight train to Rome, hoping for better weather. All we could talk about were gelato and pizza and the Colosseum.

The train breezed into Rome early in the morning, and we hauled our tired, sore bodies out onto the platform. Then we realized we hadn't brought a map and had no idea where the station was located.

"Let's just start walking," Kiska said.

Food stands dotted every street corner; souvenirs shone from every other storefront window. But we were seeking something different, something unique. We didn't know what. The whole day was ahead of us. We weren't due back at the station until that night, for the overnight train to Munich, the next stop on our whirlwind trip.

We noticed some ruins and headed for them, hefting our backpacks higher on our backs. It was a series of columns—or half columns—spread haphazardly on a small plateau, overlooking streets and a few buildings. Some tourists sat on one of the fallen stones, poring over a travel guide.

"Oh my God," I breathed.

"What?" said Kiska, coming up next to me.

I laughed and pointed. "It looks like we found the Colosseum." She followed my finger and broke into a smile. The Colosseum snoozed below us. It was early enough in the morning that the crowds hadn't rallied outside its doors. Vendors were just setting up their stands of miniature Colosseums, postcards and trinkets. We headed toward it, feeling like we had bumped into an old friend.

> We headed toward the Colosseum, feeling like we had bumped into an old friend.

"How cool is this?" Kiska asked. "We just happen to come across the Colosseum? I love Italy!"

"I think this calls for a celebration," I said.

"Gelato?"

"Perfect."

Kiska remembered a lot of great *gelaterie* near the Spanish Steps, so we took off in that general direction through the winding streets, relying on our innate navigational skills and good luck. We came across two middle-aged, well-dressed couples—Americans by the look of their polo shirts and white tennis shoes—who were arguing over a spread-out map and pointing in ten different directions.

"Excuse me," one of the men said, waving at us, "do you think you two can help us?"

"Sure!" we chirped, delighted to be able to help someone with directions. It made us feel like natives. The man smiled and pushed his Ray-Ban sunglasses up on his head. "We're looking for the Spanish Steps, but we can't figure out this map and don't know where we're even at."

"Hey, that's where we're headed," Kiska said, as he handed her the map. Both of us trailed our fingers along the pink, drawn streets, rolling the Italian names around in our mouths.

"No problem," I said.

The couples gratefully followed us, and the man with the Bans started asking us about school and our hometowns and how long we had been in Italy.

"Have you had gelato yet?" asked Kiska. "You haven't lived until you've tried it. It's awesome."

"That's what we're looking for now," I told him. "Can't beat it on a nice day like today."

He chuckled. "We'll have to do that. So what do you have planned for the rest of your time here in Rome?"

"We're only here for the day, and we've seen all of the sites before, so..." I looked at Kiska and she shrugged. "Guess we'll see what happens!"

Soon enough, we arrived at the Spanish Steps. Hundreds of people were in the square, some just lying on the steps, others eating or talking. Musicians played for coins, and a vendor was blowing balloons.

We bought gelato—a scoop of chocolate, a scoop of tiramisu, and a scoop of stracciatella, topped with whipped cream for each of us—and took a place on the steps.

"This is the perfect day," Kiska said.

"And perfect weather."

"Why couldn't Nice have been this ... nice?"

I smirked. "Nice cliché. But I know what you mean. I was looking forward to the beach. Oh, wait a minute!" I rummaged through my bag and pulled out the map of Europe that came with our rail tickets. "Let's look for a beach," I said.

Kiska leaned over the map. "You mean, a beach in Italy?"

"Sure," I said, "Why not? We have a rail ticket, we don't have to leave for Munich until tonight, and Rome is pretty close to the ocean." I looked through all of the rail stops along the beach. "How about this one? It's called Civitavecchia. That means Old City, I think. It looks like it's on the ocean." I pulled out the train schedule for the Rome station. "It's only an hour's ride from here," I said, pointing to the time chart.

Kiska smiled. "Okay. Do you know anything about it?"

"Nope, but that's why we're on an adventure, right?"

"Let's go!" she said, picking up my empty gelato cup and tossing it in a nearby trashcan. "It says the train leaves in forty minutes."

The train for Civitavecchia was fairly empty, and we sat by the windows, watching the quiet, spring-brown countryside roll by. Within the hour, the train pulled up to the modest wooden platform that was Civitavecchia's station. We were the only passengers who got off. Before us were a few shops, some not even open, and behind the shops, a stretch of perfect, empty beach. Kiska and I dumped our backpacks onto a bench near the sand and stared out into the ocean.

"This is what a beach is supposed to be like," I said.

The sand glistened like faint crystals in the midafternoon sunlight, and the water, a deep turquoise color where it met the horizon, lapped the sand with pale-blue, frothy kisses. A seagull crooned overhead. I felt my cheeks, which were toasty in the heat.

"Let's get into our suits," Kiska said.

I looked around, trying to spot a public restroom or a changing room or even a rock to hide behind.

"Where are we going to change?"

She smiled and shrugged.

"You've got to be kidding me," I protested. "Someone might see us!"

"Who?" She looked around. "We have this place all to ourselves. Besides, this is supposed to be an adventure." Kiska dug into her bag, sifted through her underwear and soiled T-shirts, and finally pulled out her bikini. "Come on."

Why not? We *were* young; we might as well be daring! So there, in the April Italian afternoon, we stripped, the salty breeze and warm light shocking our ghost-white limbs. Without towels, we just spread out on the beach, burrowing our feet in the sand and putting bunched up T-shirts under our heads.

"Now, *this* is a spring break!"

I laughed. "You know what will be the perfect ending to this day?"

"What?" Kiska murmured, nestling into the sand, bathing her back in the sun.

"Gelato."

She smiled. "Definitely."

COURTNEY MCDERMOTT, *a native of New Hampton, Iowa, and recent graduate of Mt. Holyoke College, was born with wanderlust. She thinks that all places can be judged by the quality of their food (or drink). An aspiring writer, Courtney recently dropped out of graduate school to pursue the writing lifestyle—which means little money, lots of travel and a library card.*

CARTOLINA POSTALE

*I never travel
without my diary.
One should always have
something sensational
to read on the train.
- Oscar Wilde*

Cinque Terre

Italy

Monterosso
Vernazza
Corniglia
Manarolo
Riomaggiore

The Cinque Terre

Cinque Terre

Shirts Off
for Bill and Ted

julie vick

In the high-school locker room, I was a master of a shirt change that involved leaving my bare skin exposed for only two seconds at a time. (Luckily, we didn't shower after gym class, so the only obstacle I had to overcome was changing my clothes.) I would stand facing the locker and balance my clean shirt on one knee. Then I would remove my arms from the sleeves of the shirt I was wearing, reach my arms out through the bottom of the shirt, and put my arms through the new shirt. In one quick movement, I would pull the new shirt over my head as I simultaneously pulled off the old shirt.

I had friends who were proponents of this changing method, but I also had a friend who would whip off her shirt and stand there talking to me, wearing only a bra. This, of course, only made me nervous as I searched for somewhere to look other than at her exposed skin, and it was all I could do not to say, "For the love of God, I won't be able to hear a word you are saying about what happened in geometry until you get some clothes on."

I generally tried to keep my bare-skin exposure to a minimum, both in locker rooms and in foreign countries.

....

I mention my tendency toward extreme modesty only to demonstrate just how much wine I must have consumed before agreeing to go skinny-dipping with strangers on the Italian Riviera. Sure, I had graduated from college and become a little more comfortable with nudity, but I still generally tried to keep my bare-skin exposure to a minimum, both in locker rooms and in foreign countries.

The strangers were two Brits and one American that my friend Vanessa and I had met in a hostel on the Cinque Terre, a string of five cities on the Italian coast. I can't tell you the strangers' real names because, somewhere into our fourth bottle of wine, one of our new friends decided we should all make up fake names to call each other by. We called the American Watkins G. and the two Brits Hank and Annie. They were calling Vanessa and me Bill and Ted. After finishing off most of a bottle of Chianti myself, I thought the fake names were hilarious. Especially since Annie was a guy and Bill and Ted were girls. I mean, imagine, a British man we barely knew was letting us call him Annie. (There were reasons behind all of these names, which I have since forgotten.)

Perhaps it was my pseudonym, as much as the wine, that helped me agree to go skinny-dipping. We all walked down to a very dark beach, took off our clothes, got in the cold water briefly, and then got out. I don't remember being able to see much of anything, but I do remember being glad that we had survived a drunken swim, when I woke up the next morning and reflected on what we had done.

That reflection had come with the clear, sober light of day as we hiked along a path at the top of some very tall cliffs that dropped down to some very big waves that struck some very sharp rocks. After our bonding night of drinking and swimming, we had all set out in the thick August heat for a hike on the walking path that connects the Cinque Terre. The trail edges along the Italian coast, and the path from the first city to the last is about 10 miles long. We weren't very long into the hike before I felt my shirt clinging to my back with sweat; the others were struggling with the same issue.

Watkins G. pulled off his shirt, and Vanessa and I did, too, hiking in our swimsuit tops and shorts. I wouldn't have done it in the States, but I was in Europe, with people who couldn't remember my real name, and it was hot. It was suffocatingly hot. I tried to focus on the scenery to take my mind off of it. The blue water below us sparkled in the sun and cradled rows of brightly colored boats. The little villages we walked through were dotted with pastel-colored houses and cobblestone streets. It was like a scene on a postcard you get in the middle of winter from someone gallivanting around Europe, one that really does make you wish you were there.

We were halfway between two of the towns when clouds rolled in and the lightning started. I thought I knew what to do in lightning storms: Get away from trees and other tall objects, and find a ditch to lie in. But, as it was, we were on the top of a cliff with trees all around us and no ditches in sight. We couldn't see where the trail led next as it rounded corners along the coast, but we knew we were far from the next town. We heard loud thunder strikes all around us and started counting off the time between each flash of lightning and the corresponding boom. *One, one thousand ... two, one thousand ... three, one thousand.* Each count represented a mile, the distance between the lightning strike and us. At least, that's what someone had told me in elementary school, and I had no better knowledge to go on at the time.

When we couldn't even get through the first "one thousand" before a thunderclap hit, we picked a spot to stop and wait out the storm. I thought: *I could die here on a mountain in Italy in a lightning storm. In my swimsuit. With people who've been calling me Ted.* It didn't make sense. After a while longer, Annie and Hank wanted to push on because they had to catch a train to Paris in the last town. The storm hadn't let up, but we were huddling near trees, so moving didn't seem like a bad idea. We walked out into an opening and saw telephone poles lining the trail as it climbed higher. This seemed like a worse option than cowering in the trees, so we returned to the trees to cower. I told myself it was possible to survive being hit by lightning. You could make it through it. Some people have even been hit more than once—the Guinness Book of Records holder had been hit, like, seven times. But the storm eventually passed, and, once the skies looked clear enough, we emerged from the shade of the trees and out onto the open trail.

When we walked into the next town, people were going about their business as usual. The outdoor cafés were bustling, and street vendors were selling colorful vegetables and fruit. Back in civilization, my first thought was that I should put on my shirt to cover up my swimsuit top. But, as I looked around, no one in the town seemed to be gawking at my excessive display of skin. In fact, they hardly seemed to notice us at all. I thought we may have some harried looks on our faces from our recent brush with death, but apparently we just looked like the usual tourists who didn't draw more than a glance. I was on a remote section of the Italian coast for the first, and maybe only, time in my entire life. I didn't bother putting on my shirt.

I wish I could say I kept in touch with the people Vanessa and I met in Italy, but I didn't. I saw only a small snapshot of their lives. I can see the ephemeral quality of those couple of days now, but I didn't pause to ponder the philosophical meaning of it all that afternoon. I was too caught up in forward motion as we reached the train station in town and said goodbye to Hank and Annie. Then Watkins G. and Vanessa and I went off in search of a new trail to the next town.

JULIE VICK *is a writer of sorts living in Denver, Colorado. She has hauled an often-overstuffed backpack through Europe, Asia and Latin America. Her writing has appeared in U.S. News and World Report,* The Christian Science Monitor *and McSweeney's.*

Monterosso

Ligurian Daydream

ryan daniels

"**a** glass of vintage Sciacchetrà," I ordered while gazing out along the shimmering sea of topless sunbathers. "But sir, this is your ninth glass," the *cameriere* said. "Make it so, Giovanni, make it so," I waved.

I had not a care in the world. The blinding glare off the Mar Ligure appeared as though it were an ocean of glorious sparkling gems. The sun was shining, the air smelled of wildflowers and fresh garlic, the wind playfully tickled my hair, and the sound of straw sweeping cobblestones lightly grazed my ears. I looked behind me to see an old woman hunched over her broom, clearing sand from the *piazza*.

"Your wine, sir," I heard over the increasingly audible noise.

"Yes, delightful, how much do I owe you?"

"Monterosso al Mare."

"Sorry, what was that?" I said, twitching a bit in my seat.

"Monterosso, Monterosso al Mare."

It's such a beautiful state, that ethereal moment of half consciousness when reality works its way into your dreams: when an alarm clock can become a ringing telephone, a sweeping woman a train, and an Italian waiter the conductor of the train about to pass my stop. I grabbed all of my things from the overhead and struggled toward the door. Still wiping the sleep from my eyes and the dream from my mind, I found myself on the platform. I hadn't made any plans or arranged any sort of accommodation, but, looking around me, it didn't seem that would be a problem. I was the only person who had gotten off the train.

It was March, rainy and cold, with a terrible loom of gray over the inlet of Monterosso, the largest town in Cinque Terre. Certainly not the same sunny Italian Riviera town I had seen in pictures and read about in guidebooks. But, I knew what to expect. It was part of my reason for coming: The skies might not be clear in March, but the streets sure are. On my way to town, the only moving thing I saw was an orange alley cat. I decided to follow it. These are the risks you take when you have no direction or real agenda.

The cat brought me right to the doorstep of an open *gelateria*. As I peeked in and opened the door, an old man popped up from behind the counter, scaring the *hell* out of me. I must have caught him off guard, too, both with my presence and with my ordering of three scoops of chocolate on a day like today.

"Best gelato in all Italia," the old man gloated.

"We'll see!" I said. "I've had some pretty good ones."

"Yes, but this is homemade! Forget about chocolate; here, try this special one." Handing over a cup with a single scoop of pale yellow, he announced, "Limoncino! Come, I have the bottle!"

Before I could say a thing, he took me outside and around the corner to a Realtor's office. The rain had picked up a bit, the drops making impressions as they landed in my gelato.

"Please, inside, this is miserable," said the old man.

"Thank you; is this your office?"

"Yes, of course! This is why I brought you here. You need a place to stay, don't you?"

Caught off guard, I replied, "Yes, I do, actually."

"Please sit and be comfortable. We will drink Limoncino, and then I will take you to your apartment."

"What luck I have," I thought, gazing out at the terrible weather. "A Realtor and an ice-cream man all in one!"

I had just finished the last bite of the gelato when

the old man returned with a bottle, two glasses, and a huge smile on his face.

"You know, you're early," he said. "The tourists usually come for the sun and the beach, not the rain. What made you choose to come here now?"

"Well, to see it without all the tourists," I said. "For me, the best way to capture a place and the people who live there is to see it during a time like this."

The old man sat and thought. "This is very fine Limoncino, my grandfather's recipe," he said, changing the subject. "You have to peel the lemon just right, making sure there is no pith showing. Then, leave it to dissolve for one week. I can't tell you the next step because it's secret, but after a month in the cellar, perfection! Here, have a glass."

I finished the glass entirely, and not a second after I put it on the table, the old man offered another.

....

I took a sip. Having tried several varieties of Limoncino before, I could say that this was something special. It tasted like a warm lemonade smoothie, and it felt almost healthy going down. I finished the glass entirely, and not a second after I put it on the table, the old man offered another.

"Here," he said, putting a newly filled glass in my hand. "Maybe it will brighten up the day so you can capture this beautiful place like you said. In the summer, I go up into the hills and tend to my vineyard, and every year make wine by hand. It is what my father did, and what I had hoped my son would do, but he now lives in Roma with his wife. All the young people have left. Now, no one wants to climb up the steep stairs or do the backbreaking work it takes to tend to the vineyards. We are a dying breed."

"That's a shame," I said, not really knowing which way to take the conversation.

"Yes, it is, but it is hard to blame anyone. The people here make more money off the tourists in a few months than they would if they made wine all year. Not to mention it is incredibly physical work, even for a young man like you. Here, take another glass of Limoncino. I will be right back."

There was no way I could drink another glass. The only thing I had eaten all day was that gelato, which was made with alcohol. I hadn't even seen the town yet; getting drunk would only hinder me from doing so. When the old man returned a few minutes later, he brought a space heater, a bottle of golden yellow wine, and an even bigger smile than before.

"Is this one of the wines that you made?" I asked, hoping not to invite a sample.

"Yes, of course! It is Sciacchetrà, made from the sweet juice of grapes right before they turn into raisins. I even designed the label myself!" The old man handed me the bottle.

"*Sogno a occhi aperti Ligure*," I read aloud. "What does that mean?"

"It means Ligurian daydream. That is for you, for

tonight. Come now; we will go to your apartment. I must warn you, however, that there is no heat. But I have this for you," he said, tapping the heater with a smile.

We headed back out into the rain. Weaving through the alleyways and stopping under the arches for cover, we finally crossed the main *piazza*, which looked right out onto the Ligurian Sea. Several boats were docked in the harbor, and even more on the beach.

"This is Piazza Colombo, named after *Cristoforo*," the old man said, stopping for a minute. "Sometimes, I like to sit and just watch the boats dance back and forth with the ocean, but today is no day for that. Come, the apartment is just up this way."

I imaged how everything must look in the summer, the boats replaced by sunbathers and swimmers, the sounds of rain drops becoming sounds of bustling people. I took a deep breath of fresh rain and saltwater air, and everything became calm and desolate again, not another person in sight.

When we finally reached the apartment, I was fully soaked. I put my backpack down and took the tour. "The bathroom is there, the kitchen is there, and the bedroom is there," the old man said, pointing every which direction. "Now go change out of your wet clothes, and I will put the heater on."

When I went into the bedroom to change, I noticed all sorts of personal effects lying on the dresser and end tables: pictures of people, an old pocket watch leaning against a lamp, jewelry, and old lira notes lying in a silver tray. I then looked in the dresser drawers and found them filled with clothes. He had given me his apartment. I finished dressing and came out to find the old man fiddling with the oven.

"This has only a little gas, but it should work just fine," he said.

"Thank you," I replied. "Is this your apartment that you're giving me?"

"Yes, but I have another behind the office." He smiled. "Like I said before, there is more money to be made off the tourists than off the wine."

"Well, thank you," I said with slight regret. "You've been very kind to me, and thank you also for the wine."

"I will come by tomorrow, and if it is nice out, I can show you where it came from."

"I would like that very much. Thank you—" I paused. He had been so cordial and friendly that a formal introduction hadn't come up. I extended my hand and introduced myself.

He shook it, and, with a great big smile, said, "Giovanni."

RYAN DANIELS *has traveled to more than 40 countries and lived on three continents. After driving across the Sahara Desert and taking on the Mindanao Sea by canoe, he now calls the jungles of New York his home.*

Riomaggiore

The Way of Love

ryan forsythe

knowing I would be in Italy for a few days, I asked my friend Antonio where I could get away from big crowds of people. No, I'd never seen the Vatican or the canals of Venice. I hadn't seen the ancient ruins of Rome or the Leaning Tower of Pisa. But in backpacking around Europe, there was one thing I definitely had seen: other backpackers. Lots of them. And now I needed a break.

Antonio thought for a moment. "In November, it won't be crowded at the Cinque Terre. I would go there." I had no idea what he was talking about.

The Cinque Terre, he told me, were five small fishing villages, connected by a walkway overlooking the Ligurian Sea. He noted that it was quite romantic, with the water to one side, and trees, flowers and quaint homes to the other. I wasn't worried about romance, I told him. I planned to be alone.

I stepped off the train in Riomaggiore, the first of the five towns. Not knowing where this walkway was, I examined a map at the train station. I spotted what I assumed was the path: It was labeled "*Via dell'amore*," which my high-school Latin skills quickly translated for me as "the Way of Love." That had to be it. What else would you call a romantic little path wending through small villages? From the map, it appeared that the walkway was just around the corner. But I studied the streets a little longer to see what else was in town, and to make sure there was no other romantic walking path. Then I heard a voice behind me, speaking Italian. I turned around and found a young woman staring at me, a maroon scarf wrapped beneath brunette hair.

"Do you speak English?" I asked.

"Uh ... yes." She paused and thought for a second. "Do you know ... the way to ... the *Villa dell'amore*?"

"The Way of Love?" I asked. And then, in the cheesiest faux-debonair voice I could muster, I said, "I know it well. Care to join me?"

She smiled and blushed, but nodded. Yes, in less than one minute, I had abandoned my plan to get some me-time. But hey, my girlfriend was back in Ohio, and I was suddenly lonely with no one to talk to. Except for Dominique.

As we walked, I learned she was from Quebec but was studying art and Italian in Florence. Her native tongue was French, but she remembered a fair bit of English from school days. She was taking a break from Florence to see the Cinque Terre.

We strolled along, stopping occasionally to smell flowers, view the cliffs down to the water, or wave to the locals in Manarola, the second of the five villages. Over the course of three hours, we saw only two other backpackers, with whom we chatted briefly.

As we walked on a small beach in Corniglia, the third town, Dominique decided it was time to turn back. We had stopped to chat periodically, and it soon would be dark.

> I wanted to see the remaining two villages, but, even more, I wanted to continue the conversation.

I wanted to see the remaining two villages, but, even more, I wanted to continue the conversation. "I should probably head back, too," I said. And then, thinking she might take me for some crazy stalker guy, I added, "I have to catch a train."

We were still talking and laughing when we made it back to Riomaggiore under the cover of night. Dominique suggested we check the station for the train schedule. But I didn't want to leave so soon.

"Actually, I'm pretty hungry," I said. "I should probably eat something first. Care to join me for dinner?"

She smiled.

At a nearby trattoria, we found a grand total of two other diners, nearly in each other's laps, oblivious to our presence. Sitting down, I realized it was Thanksgiving back in Ohio. But this menu offered no hint of turkey or stuffing or pumpkin pie. Instead, we enjoyed pizza with *salame* and *funghi* and red wine. Not quite what the pilgrims ate.

The owner came by every now and then to chat with Dominique in Italian. Once, he motioned to the other couple while he spoke, and then pointed at us. My dinner partner blushed, making it clear the man had suggested that, by the time we left, we would be just like them.

She told him it could never happen; she was from Quebec and I was from Ohio. But the owner remained hopeful. He pointed at the man in the corner and said commandingly, "Ohio," and then at the woman in his lap: "Quebec."

When we finally left the restaurant, the train station was dark. No more trains tonight, I thought.

Dominique suggested we ask the man who had rented a room to her if he had another available. He did, he told us, motioning for us to follow him. Down the street and up some stairs we went. Right before he opened the door to the room, I heard Dominique say to herself, a little surprised, "This is my room."

Sure enough, her backpack was on one bed. But there was another bed in the room.

"Is okay?" the man asked, smiling.

I looked at her. "Are you okay with this? I could find another place. ... "

"No," she said. "It's okay."

Not quite ready to sleep, we played cards while sharing more stories of our lives. Then Dominique decided it was time for a French lesson. Mostly she focused on fruits, but then she taught me a few phrases. The first was *"Veux-tu avoir une aventure avec moi?"* She said that if a woman ever said this to me, I should respond, *"Oui, j'aime les femmes exotiques!"*

We practiced a few times before she translated for me: "Would you like to have an adventure with me?" A euphemism, she told me. And the answer: "Yes, I like exotic women."

Sure, I like exotic woman. But not enough to forget so soon about that girlfriend back in Ohio. We slept in our separate beds.

The next morning, I was preparing to leave when Dominique said, "Would you care to join me for the day?" She wasn't even sure where she would go, but that didn't bother me.

"That sounds great," I said.

We hopped the train to nearby Sestri Levante, and passed a slow day strolling the town—taking photographs, eating bread and cheese, hanging out on the beach. I learned more French, as well as her secret recipe for lemon ice cream. But then it was time to move on.

As the train slowed to a halt back in Riomaggiore,

there was just enough time for a kiss on the cheek goodbye before she hopped out and the train started moving again. We continued smiling and waving as the distance between us increased. I think I detected a tear in her eye, but it could have been dirt on the train window.

Back in Ohio, my girlfriend and I broke up (I think it was mutual). A month after that, I received an e-mail containing one short phrase: "*Veux-tu avoir une aventure avec moi?*"

I hit reply: "*Oui, j'aime les femmes exotiques!*"

When the train departed Riomaggiore that day, I had no idea if I'd ever see Dominique again. But seven months later, I flew to see her in Quebec, and we picked up where we'd left off in the Cinque Terre.

Only now I didn't have a girlfriend.

RYAN FORSYTHE *was born in Cleveland, Ohio. He once took a 5,000-mile road trip in a little yellow school bus named Lola. He now lives in Redwood National Park, where he and his wife, Kaci, manage Redwood Hostel and their son, Rory. In his spare time, he writes children's books (for adults). He is the author of "The Little Veal Cutlet That Couldn't."*

Cinque Terre

Mirages

jeffrey james keyes

Waiting for a train to the next town in the Cinque Terre, I was sitting, sketching people on the other side of the tracks. Then I saw the mirage. I stopped drawing and wrote in my sketchbook, in big letters: "I am officially going crazy. I have started seeing actual mirages because of the heat."

I had been backpacking for a few weeks now, after a long semester in London, and had made it through La Spezia to the Cinque Terre, where I planned to spend a week hiking and exploring. There was this girl in my London program named Rachel; I'd had the biggest crush on her but never got up the nerve to ask her out. Then, at our farewell party at our London school, we shared a drink and she confessed that she was upset our paths hadn't crossed earlier. We both agreed we should meet again when we got back to the States, but there I was, weeks later, still unable to forget that night and our conversation. I had dreams about her. I couldn't stop thinking of her.

And here, across the tracks from me at this train station, was a mirage of her. It was actually calling my name. "You're not real!" I shouted out across the tracks. "You're only a mirage!" Great, I thought, I have officially lost my marbles.

The mirage beckoned me to come over to its side of the tracks. There was a fly walking on my knee. I could feel the sensation, so I guessed that I wasn't seeing things. It was her. She was real. I put my sketchbook away, zipped up my backpack, and carried it across the tracks. We embraced, and we both knew at once that this was the moment we'd been waiting for. We didn't have to wait until we got back home; we could start to get to know each other here, in this serendipitous moment.

Rachel was staying near the Riomaggiore train station at Mama Rosa's hostel, in a cheaper room than mine. So, I checked out of my hotel in Manarola and came over to meet Mama Rosa, who was sunning herself in a lawn chair. She was elated that Rachel had brought her a customer, so she gave Rachel a break on her room as she checked me in. We ate a brief lunch at the hostel—Rachel had picked up a baguette and some goat cheese, and we shared some chocolates that I had brought from Switzerland. They were so melted and messy from my travels, I got chocolate all over my shirt and had to change into something clean. I noticed her watching me as I changed, but I didn't mind.

The rest of the day was like the beginning of our honeymoon. We left our tour books at the hostel and explored things on our own, hiking from town to town. I picked a gorgeous violet flower and gave it to her; we bought pesto from a woman who said that pesto originated in this region.

Later on, it began to drizzle, so we took shelter in Vernazza. When the rain stopped, we walked out on the docks and found the most amazing little jellyfish on the ground. We returned home together

> **The rest of the day was like the beginning of our honeymoon.**

that night and played cards on a big wooden table at Mama Rosa's. I leaned over the table and kissed her, making "us" a reality.

The next few days we spent like lovebirds: sitting on rocks and watching the water; hiking back to Vernazza to climb the tower (Mama Rosa told us we had to); eating pesto, fish, pizza, cheese and Nutella with the local breads. I sketched Rachel sleeping in the sun; we drank delicious red wine and ate amazing pasta at night. We visited the baroque church in San Lorenzo.

On our fourth day, we decided to travel to Florence

together. Neither of us had seen Michelangelo's sculpture of David, so we agreed we would find it together. From there, we had to go our separate ways.

We started our search in Signoria Square, but a local informed us that we were viewing one of the many David copies scattered around the city. It took us almost two more hours to find the real one, and secretly I knew that we were stalling to stretch out our time together. But finally, we found the Academia. We stood beside each other, gazing at Michelangelo's grand marble beauty. We both had tears in our eyes. I tried to make it seem like mine were from awe at Michelangelo's masterpiece, but Rachel saw right through it.

We embraced in front of the statue and then said goodbye. I was going to meet a friend in a remote part of Tuscany; she was off to Venice. We agreed to meet up in the States. This time, it felt as if we were planning on it.

At the end of my trip, I returned home to New York City. After graduation, Rachel moved to New York, and we started dating. Now it's four years later, and I plan to propose to her. If she says yes, I'm going to suggest we return to the Cinque Terre. I wonder if Mama Rosa is still around. Maybe she can find us a honeymoon suite.

JEFFREY JAMES KEYES *lives in New York and writes poems, plays and short stories. He won a 2005 Hizza Award for his play "3 A.M. Jelly Belly Hookup." His play "Orange Alert" was a semifinalist in the Strawberry Festival in 2005. He recently completed his first full-length play, "Iphigenia in Williamsburg," and is now developing "Wentworth Avenue." He received his B.A. from Fordham University in 2002 and has been working as an actor, writer and yoga teacher ever since.*

CARTOLINA POSTALE

Traveling is like gambling ...
generally where it is
least expected we receive,
more or less than what
we hoped for.
- Johann von Goethe

Firenze
&Toscana

san Gimignano • *Firenze*
• *Siena*

Italy

Florence

Worth Every Euro

lainey seyler

It was 10:30 at night in Florence, and Myra and I still needed a place to stay. We were standing outside a centuries-old building, gazing in bewilderment at the occupants' directory—family apartments, businesses, hostels, each with a button to buzz their rooms—and wondering which button to push.

"I think that is the Italian word for hostel." I pointed to a button marked "*ostello*," recalling our last search for lodgings in Venice. We pressed the button and crossed our fingers, hoping that whomever we disturbed would not be upset because we woke them or their children. Maybe whoever answered could give us a closet with a lock where we could sleep. The response to the buzzer was just a click releasing the door lock. We looked at each other, shrugged, pushed open the door, and made our way up a very dark and very narrow staircase.

When we found all the first-floor doors closed, we turned to climb the second flight of stairs. At the top, a door was ajar. We knocked, and the Italian version of the mother from "My Big Fat Greek Wedding" greeted us, plump and friendly. She had dark, rough skin and permed, dyed hair that was supposed to be blond but was instead orangey. It was an overwhelmingly popular style among middle-aged Italian women.

She welcomed us into her house, which looked more like a vaulted Benedictine monastery than a hotel. As she informed us that she was full for the night but knew of another place we could stay, her 16-year-old daughter ventured into the room. She was a beautiful, younger and smaller version of her mother. She could speak English well enough to ask the typical questions: "Where are you from? Where are you going? Do you like Italy?"

We should have been at ease knowing we had a place to sleep for the night. But all the warnings from the travel guidebooks flashed through my head:

Do not agree to stay somewhere without seeing it first.

Do not agree to a room without knowing the price.

Do not follow someone to their "hostel."

Do not get into an unmarked taxi.

While we waited in their dim entryway, visions of being taken to a Mafia-owned brothel crept into my overactive imagination. A door opened two flights below and someone small ascended the stairs.

The woman wore four-inch cork-soled sandals, and she could not have been more than 5 feet tall. Her hair was red and thinning, most likely from overprocessing; it looked as if she, too, had gone dye-crazy attempting to shed the years. She looked like a lifelong smoker who'd consistently chosen cigarettes over spaghetti. Her neon green jumper was noticeably large on her, emphasizing her frail frame.

After gossiping for a few minutes with her friend, she ordered us to follow her out the door and down the stairs. She walked with an espresso-fueled bounce, talking to us half in unintelligible Italian, half in English: "Stay close, mozzarella, we are very near, lasagna, hurry, hurry, spaghetti *capellini*, you are lucky I found you, *uno, due*, you will like the room."

> **The further we went, the more I wondered if we would ever be able to find our way out of that maze.**

We race-walked to keep up with her, darting across streets and down alleys. The further we went, the more I wondered if we would ever be able to find our way out of that maze.

She stopped at a door, demonstrated how to use its lock, and then pushed it open. "This is it," she said.

"How much?" I finally managed to cut in.

"Not much. It's a good price."

Myra noticed my anxiety and soothed, "It'll be fine," exaggerating the last word as if she truly believed it.

I reassured myself, *It's better than a park bench. We only have to stay one night. It'll be okay. Breathe.* Once we got inside, she stopped again to show us the locks on the door. "Okay, this is important. The locks are very important."

"One." She pushed a lever at the foot of the door. "Two." She latched a deadbolt. "Three." She reached on tip-toe and clicked a lock closed higher on the door. "I will show you again. One, two, three. Now you try." Myra took her place and proceeded to engage all three deadbolts. Then it was my turn. All this while, the woman stopped talking only to take a breath.

Once we had passed the entrance exam, she ushered us into our room. We walked through the bathroom, between the shower and the toilet, before stepping into the bedroom. The sparseness of the furniture accentuated how big and empty the room was. We could see that she had received the call from her friend in this room, and she had left in such a hurry that she had forgotten to turn off the 12-inch black-and-white television. A newspaper was lying open on the table.

She quickly changed the sheets on the bed while Myra and I sat at the table and I secretly took a video with my digital camera (I had to get documented proof of her existence). The bed was little more than a twin, but after eyeing the well-worn mattress on the floor, I decided to take my chances with Myra. The wardrobe smelled like urine, and, through the open windows, which looked out onto a tin roof, we could hear a man snoring upstairs. When we closed them, the room was too hot. I spent the entire night clinging to the edge of the bed, facing the wall, trying not to make body contact or awaken to find myself breathing on Myra's face. But for 60 euros a night, we decided it wasn't worth moving.

We woke up early the next day, looking forward to the showers we had gone without at the last hostel. Wearing my plastic flip-flops, I stepped around the basin found in every private Italian bathroom and into the shower. I was too afraid to ever ask the purpose of this mystery bedpan contraption, and even more afraid to touch it.

As I shampooed my hair, I heard a knock on the door. "Myra!" I shouted, "Someone is at the door."

Myra passed through the bathroom to answer the door. It was Madam, as Myra had decided to call her, wondering if we were going to stay another night. Apparently she had noticed Myra clipping her fingernails out of the window, and had rushed over to greet us for the day and ask about our plans.

"We decided to stay two more nights," said Myra.

"Okay, a couple on honeymoon has that room the second night. But no problem, no problem. I will move them," said Madam. "They have not called. You are good girls. Do not worry."

"Well, uh, are you sure? We could move."

"No, no, no. Do not worry. You want coffee? I have coffee."

"Yes!" I piped from my place behind the shower curtain.

"Okay. Five minutes. I have coffee."

I had just enough time to dry off and get dressed before Madam was back with a steel stovetop espresso maker and a miniature tea set placed on a silver tray. She poured two thimble-sized cups of espresso for Myra and me, and left us to take care of the sugar, which I now know we were fortunate to get at all.

The espresso had bite. We could take only teeny sips, instead of shooting it down the way I was used to drinking coffee back home. But it packed caffeine, and that's all I cared about.

Before we left to do the usual sightseeing, Madam sat down with us to ask about our plans for the day and warn us about the dangers of the city. She made certain that we didn't leave without an umbrella, and she greeted us when we came home that night and the next.

Madam was our one real connection to that city of red tiled roofs and screeching mopeds. And she took care of us like a nosy, worried, loving mother. Well worth the €60 per night.

LAINEY SEYLER *spent a semester exploring Spain and the rest of Europe. She returned home with a closetful of souvenirs, no money, a healthy coffee addiction, and an itch for more travel. Upon graduation from college, she will be pursuing her career path of vagabonding, starting as an English teacher in Thailand.*

Florence

Coffee Shop
Lessons

sarah naimark

as a woman, sitting alone in a public place is like standing outside in a lightning storm: you could be placing yourself in the path of whatever's about to strike. But sitting alone in Italy is like waving a metal rod over your head—you're just plain asking for it.

Traveling by myself in Florence meant I spent many nights sitting alone, and I'd come to enjoy the local restaurants and cafés in peaceful solitude. I did what I could to remain alone, always bringing a book, a newspaper, or letters to write, so I could avoid intrusive stares and probing questions. Sitting alone was one of the few times in this foreign land when I didn't feel lost, overwhelmed or confused by what was happening around me.

This stormy night, I aimed my umbrella for the clean, bright interior of Edison, a four-story bookstore and café off Piazza Repubblica in the center of Florence. I always bypassed the snootier, more commercial cafés. I shook off the rainwater and marched up the spiral staircases to the café level, where I was delighted to find an open table amid the usual masses of noisily content espresso-drinkers. Tea ordered, rain jacket peeled off, I settled in for an uneventful night of writing letters to loved ones.

"Free?" I heard the raspy question before I looked up to see who asked it. He was probably just short of 70, with cropped, gray-white hair, a heavy gold bracelet, two gold rings and a platinum necklace. Thick, silver hair covered the arm he was pointing at the empty chair across from me. I nodded reluctantly and pulled my stack of letters closer to the edge. Tables were hot commodities at Edison, and I thought I'd perfected the technique of spreading my things all over the table to discourage eager conversationalists.

My vanilla tea had just begun to brew, and I could already smell its thick aroma. A few drops sloshed over my cup's rim as the man plunked down in the chair opposite mine. He brought no coffee, no book. These were not the things he came to Edison for, apparently. I picked up my pen again, and restarted the sentence he had interrupted. He leaned back into the metal chair—a slick, languid pose that didn't quite suit his rough appearance. He proffered his hand from all the way across the round table.

"My name is Anton," he began. "Not Sant'Antonio. I don't have miracles! You know! I have not miracles!" He grinned broadly and shifted back further in his seat. I smiled in spite of the distraction from my letter and gave him my name.

"Sarah...that's a nice name," Anton said. "Short, easy to remember." I couldn't disagree, so I turned back to my writing. He bent his head low and cocked it, forcing me to look up and make eye contact. To break the strange silence, I asked him what he did for a living.

"Nothing," he chortled. "I am *vagabondo*. My mother, she said to me when I am born, she said, 'My dear son, you are born to sleep and live to rest!'" He smiled, self-satisfied. "I no drink, I no smoke, because drink, smoke, it make me dead. I'm going old. I just *dormire, riposare*." He was simplifying and emphasizing the Italian for me. Yeah, yeah, I thought. You "sleep" and you "rest." I learned those verbs months ago.

Other café-goers walked by us, searching for surfaces where they could perch, their cups teetering on saucers. I'm certain we looked to be an odd duo: a stocky, graying man from Naples chatting up a young American with long brown hair and a thick maroon sweater.

Anton asked what I was doing in Florence, where

I was from, how many degrees Celsius it was in San Francisco (the universal question). He spoke to me in English, and I tried to respond in Italian. When he did speak Italian, his Neapolitan accent would slush against the words I was so used to hearing in crisp Tuscan.

Giving up the pretense of writing very important letters, I took my warm porcelain cup in both hands and leaned my elbows on the table. The tea had steeped too long, and it puckered in my mouth as I sipped.

It's part of what I love best about traveling alone: You can be a hundred people.

I embellished and fogged away pieces of my story as I told it to Anton. It's part of what I love best about traveling alone: You can be a hundred people. I chose to leave out the part where I was a nanny and to focus more on the research I was conducting on behalf of a local professor.

Just that morning, I'd nearly jumped in the green Arno to quell my frustrations at the Florentine librarian who had made me feel stupid and small. My Italian had quaked and retreated under her harsh treatment, and I had left the stone library defeated, without the book on architectural modernism the professor had wanted.

But under Anton's open gaze, I easily described the nature of futurism and how it related to fascism in flowing, albeit elementary, Italian. Were these my words? Where had they been hiding?

Realizing I'd been pattering on about myself, I

asked Anton how he passed his days since retiring as a waiter.

"I wake up, I shave. I eat breakfast, sometimes I go out *per mangiare l'aria*," he replied. I did the quick translation in my head: to eat the air? I wondered if this was a common expression or one unique to Sant'Antonio. I filed that away to ask someone later.

"Don't you get bored?" I asked.

"Sarah. I say to you, I am very *pigro*, very lazy." I hadn't known that word. Filed it away. "You know, my mother say to me when I born, 'My dear son, you are born to sleep...'"

"And live to rest?" I finished. He guffawed, inviting sneers from the next table. One doesn't guffaw in Tuscany.

"That's right, baby! I don't need no thing. Except *una bella ragazza*," he sat up a bit taller in his chair. Uh-oh. I had hoped this wasn't coming. "A beautiful girl like you. You are young and studious. That is good. But me, I might be your father..." I nodded vigorously to encourage this train of thought.

"I want to find a woman, but I also want to sleep," Anton said, holding out his two palms as if they were balancing scales, weighing the pros and cons of those two options. I scanned my mind for the words "mutually exclusive" in Italian but came up short.

After a thoughtful pause, brows knit, I told him he should take out a personal ad: "*Cercasi la Bella Addormentata!*" I said this last part rather loudly, beaming with pride that I had not only recalled the proper reflexive verb "in search of," but also the folk name for Sleeping Beauty in one fell Italian swoop. My linguistic triumph didn't seem to register with Anton, who was now deep in a reflective slouch.

"But you know, Sarah, these days, ugly. The people, they are like wolf. They eat you up." He made his hands into mock claws and bared his teeth. "You must watch up, baby. You gotta watch up." He nodded solemnly as he imparted his wisdom.

We chatted a bit more, until I gathered up my unfinished letters, grabbed my cold, empty tea cup and stood. He told me I could find him there at the bookstore pretty much any night of the week, sleeping on the couches in the fiction/mystery section. Smiling, I put on the Stalin-era paperboy cap that I wouldn't have dared to wear at home. For Anton, this could be my signature look, my usual hat. I liked that thought. I tipped my hat and walked away.

I did see Anton at Edison again—and I crept by slowly as he snored lightly on the couches. I already had gotten my lesson from him. It was someone else's turn to be struck by lightning.

SARAH NAIMARK *is a Bay Area native who is currently located in Bologna, Italy, in pursuit of espresso, pecorino and a degree in international relations.*

Florence

50,000 Lire for the Room

dave prine

When the drinks reached our table for lunch that first day in Paris, Madaline's Coke was half the size and twice the price of my carafe of wine. Madaline and I weren't big drinkers, but we were on a tight budget. By the time we made it to Italy, we realized that if we wanted to save money, we'd have to lay off the soda and stick with the *vino*. And drinking wine at every meal, we rationalized, might help us pass as locals.

On our final night in Florence, we had each consumed a half-liter of wine over dinner, and we began reasoning that the more wine we drank, the more money we would save. The gods of inexpensive intoxication watched over us, and we quickly encountered our patron saint, an adorable old man with a wispy white beard and eyes that revealed a warm and welcoming heart. More importantly, he sold cheap wine. So as not to offend the gods, we quickly selected a bottle, paid the blurry man, uncorked it, and staggered off with two plastic cups, searching for a quiet place to sit down and enjoy an intimate drink.

We made it as far as the Duomo, the famous and less-than-intimate Cathedral of Florence, which was teeming with loud tourists. We found a spot on the steps and consumed the bottle within 20 minutes, leaving ourselves little else to do but talk to random tourists. After a few conversations with English speakers, we found ourselves talking with Parisians, who apparently were speaking French. Madaline and I had taken French classes together, so we decided to put our college educations to good use.

At first, things flowed smoothly ("You're from Paris? *Mon dieu*, we were just there!"), but our skills soon faltered ("I love shame. No, I mean cheese. I love cheese!"), until finally our French gave out completely ("Hey, nice goat. Can he dance?"). Madaline and I had stopped making any sense, so we excused ourselves, wished the Parisians what I can only hope meant farewell, and beat a hasty retreat to our hostel, laughing at our abortive and obnoxious attempts to speak French. We decided it was time to call it a night.

Back in our room, Madaline claimed her side of the bed and quickly fell asleep. I was lying next to her, wide awake in the dark, listening to the sounds of laughter and conversation coming from the streets below. I couldn't sleep; I was wired from all that wine in my system. After an hour, I got out of bed, doffed an imaginary hat to Madaline, and tiptoed out the door. We'd be staying in Florence only one more day, and I had to get out and see more of the city.

It was a good plan, until I reached the front door: locked for curfew. But it was 11 p.m., still fairly early, so I woke the resident manager and fabricated a story about how I urgently needed to use a pay phone. Or spatula, for all I knew. My Italian was worse than my French. He groggily but forgivingly unlocked the door, and I flew the coop. The hostel wouldn't re-open until 8 a.m., and there was no way I could return before then without feeling like a major American inconvenience. So I hatched a simple plan: Stay out all night. Armed with only my passport and an Italian phrase book, I took off into the night, ready to take on whatever Florence could throw at me. I would not flinch. I was brave. I was determined; resolute. I was drunk out of my mind.

Luckily, the night was warm and hospitable, so spending the midnight hours roaming Florence's pell-mell streets was easy, even while intoxicated. Unfortunately, most of Florence seemed to be shut down. Was this a school night? Perhaps I was simply walking in a less-happening part of town.

Had I a guidebook listing the late-night hot spots, my night would have been complete. Instead, after an hour, I found myself walking down the same horribly recognizable vacant streets again, unwittingly retracing my steps, all of which led to darkness and silence. Each time I stumbled upon an unexplored road, it led me to an equally inert part of town. Giving in to frustration and boredom, I found a well-lighted corner with a bench, sat down, pulled out my phrase book, and studied verb conjugations. *"Parlo, parli, parliamo..."* It was going to be a long night, but at least I'd learn lots of Italian. And just in time. In two days we'd be on our way to Greece.

I would have made it to past participles had an approaching car not broken the monotony. I looked up from my conjugations and watched a small car drive right by me. I might not have given it much thought, except that the car slowed down enough for me to make eye contact with the driver: an Italian. A *female* Italian. My favorite kind. She was gorgeous: She had long, black hair, and a face with eyes, a nose and a mouth. Actually, it was hard to tell exactly what she looked like in that light, and in my condition.

But she was pretty from what I could tell, and she noticed me, and that was all I needed. I could hardly wait to tell my friends back home about the gorgeous Italian woman I made eye contact with as she drove by.

Which is all she did. She just drove by.

Speechless, I stood on the corner wondering if I should kick myself. Did I just blow the opportunity of a lifetime, the chance to wave down the girl of my dreams, fall madly in love, and have my mail forwarded to Florence? No, of course not. Surely we'd move to the country, build a small cottage, and have my mail forwarded there. Occasionally we'd come back to Florence, if only to show our children where their parents met. ...

Quickly, these musings gave way to reality: I was standing alone and girl-less. I decided to stay put. She ("Florette," I named her) knew where I was. Maybe she'd come back. I decided to give her five minutes. If she hadn't returned by then, it wasn't meant to be. Four minutes later (or was it 26?) Florette zipped around the corner. This time she came to a complete stop, engine running. I had mere moments to put on the charm.

Even if I couldn't win her heart, I dared not underestimate the kindness of Europeans. Perhaps I could even finagle a couch to sleep on until morning. I approached the driver's-side window. Not only did she have a gorgeous face and long curls of tar-black hair, but she also wore the shortest skirt and sexiest fishnet stockings I'd ever seen. I had no choice but to impress her with some smooth talking, and in her native tongue, no less.

"*Uh ... you ... speak ... uh ... English?*" I asked in my best Italian.

"Yes, a little," the Italian replied haltingly.

She speaks English! Thank God! "Speak" was the only verb I could even partially conjugate. Had she come by an hour later, I could have had a more meaningful conversation involving eating, bathing, and doing laundry.

"So, uh, you stopped..."

"You stopped me." Apparently, gawking and looking confused had the power to stop gorgeous Italians. I promised myself to explore these powers to their full potential someday, but for now, it was time to move in for the kill.

"So, uh, you want to, uh... get a coffee?" *Please say yes. Please say yes.*

"Well, my time is money."

Eons passed while I deciphered her remark. She might as well have said it in Italian, or even Korean, given my reaction time. I stood there, mouth wide open, pondering her response. *What could she mean by... wait, does that mean... no, she can't possibly... boy, nice legs. ...*

"I charge 100,000 lire," she barked impatiently as she began her sales pitch. My mind raced. I was talking to my first Italian prostitute! I couldn't wait to tell my parents. "And the room will cost 50,000..."

Conversions swirled around in my brain. Italy's pre-Euro currency was one of the trickiest to convert, especially on the spot. She charges $1.50? $4,000? After several botched calculations, I guessed her offer to run about $100, including the room. I was considering all the money I hadn't budgeted for Italian hookers—even with the money I saved by drinking wine—when it occurred to me that I had brought no money at all. I'd left my wallet back in the room. So much for taking her out for a coffee, but since that was the furthest thing from Florette's mind, I was off the hook.

Before I could respond to her offer, a police car with two officers pulled up behind us. I was still the invincible traveler, impervious to anything Europe could throw my way, although that made much more sense when I was meandering the streets intoxicated an hour before. It was slowly sinking in that I—as well as my new sweetheart—could be in for some serious trouble.

Instead, Florette raced off, leaving me at the mercy of the cops.

Hopefully, Florette would tell the police a touching story about how she was on her way to buy, say, a roasting pan and a stapler, but stopped to help a lost-but-amazingly-handsome tourist find his way back to his hostel. The *polizia* would commend her compassion and selflessness, and leave us to continue "getting acquainted." Instead, Florette raced off, leaving me at the mercy of the cops. That's it, I decided. We're breaking up.

To save face, I sank to a new low: I played the Ignorant American. I approached the car and asked for directions in broken Italian while frantically flipping through my phrase book. "*No speaky Italiano. Dove il stazione del train-o? Quanto costa la spaghetti? Mach schnell!*" The cops smirked to each other and waved me away dismissively as they drove off, disappearing down one of the winding streets, leaving me feeling cheap and dirty, but free from incarceration.

So I lost the girl, but I didn't get imprisoned. As far as my European travels went, this was par for the course. Sticking around had yielded positive results (and I had nowhere else to hang for a good six hours), so I lingered on the corner. But the longer I waited, the more nothing happened. I was about to start walking when a familiar pair of headlights came toward me. Florette hadn't forgotten me after all! She pulled up next to me and tried one last time to seal the deal.

When I explained that, even if I were interested, I had only 100 lire worth of lint in my pocket, Florette quickly turned cold. Without suggesting another option, such as inviting me out for coffee or offering me a freebie, she drove off unfulfilled. Oh, well. What did I expect from an Italian prostitute, especially one with a name like Florette? Still, part of me wished she had suggested one of the alternatives. I really could've used the coffee. It was going to be a long night.

DAVE PRINE *spent a year in Tubingen, Germany, butchering the language. Since then, he has embarrassed himself in 17 countries by trying to speak the local language. His writings have appeared in* Transitions Abroad *and* The Santa Barbara Independent, *and he is working on a book of techniques for learning languages. He allegedly lives in Santa Barbara, California.*

San Gimignano

Get Us Out of the Tuscan Sun

keridwen cornelius

he San Gimignano of travel magazines is sunshine, villas the color of egg pasta, and cypresses like bottles of green olive oil, where some young man, framed by the town's dozen sienna towers rising behind him, clicks by on a rickety bicycle.

Apparently, lots of people read those stories, because when my friend Bonnie and I reached San Gimignano, it was jammed with busloads of tourists swarming around us, photographing themselves next to stuffed wild boars in the shop fronts and making a loud, collective buzzing. I sought relief in the *toiletta*, where a man shaped like a ham hock had parked himself on a stool, collecting entry fees. "A euro for a dirty hole in the ground? That's ridiculous," a woman there said to her friend, loudly enough for the man to hear.

Something about him made me suspect that the bathroom was actually free, and he'd come up with a unique method of panhandling. I gave him a don't-mess-with-me stare and marched into the stall without paying. It worked. When I emerged, Bonnie had decided on the longest of four hikes featured in her *Hiking in Tuscany* guidebook.

"Should take us about five hours," she said. The village's narrow lanes unwound down the hill, into the wide-open countryside, where the soft buzz of bees drifting in the wildflowers gradually replaced the loud buzz of conversation. Old men zipped by on Vespas. Fuzzy hills and vineyards rolled into the horizon, punctuated by cypress trees, and San Gimignano's towers got smaller with every glance back. About an hour into the hike, a group on bicycles bearing the name of a fancy tour company huffed up the hill.

"Look at that," I said smugly. "I know they paid more than $5,000 for their two-week trip, and we're on exactly the same trail."

About three hours into the hike, we sat down to a lunch of bread, cheese, wild-boar salami and a little wine. Sitting satisfied under a shady tree, post-lunch lazy, we decided to rethink our hike.

"I think it's gonna take us another four hours to do the full loop," Bonnie mused, crunching on a biscotti.

"Or we could cut across here," she said, pointing to a thin gray line on the map, "and be back in about two hours."

"I'm getting a little tired. Maybe we should do the shorter route," I said, sipping wine from a broken plastic cup. I looked more closely at the tourist office's map. "Are we sure it's actually a trail?"

"It's in the guidebook, too: *Past the large oak tree, take the unmarked trail left onto a rough path that descends into a ditch. Cross several streams, then ascend steeply through a tall forest and turn right at the broken yellow sign.*"

"You're joking."

She looked at me innocently.

"Sorry," I said to her, " the road we've been taking— is it actually a trail?"

"Not really. The lady at the tourist office said to take the main road and turn right behind the *alimentari*."

I think someone has said of the Italians, and I may paraphrase here, "They make love; they make shoes; but they cannot make trails." Maybe there *was* something to those $5,000 guided tours. But I rallied: "OK, what the heck. I'm sure we'll figure it out." So we set off to find the Thin Gray Line.

"Do you think that's it?"

"That's a river."

"Maybe it was that footpath back a ways."

"The one overgrown with gorse bushes?"

"Maybe it's further up ahead."

About an hour later, we decided that the trail had,

in fact, never existed at all. But we figured we knew the general direction we needed to go, and we could make our own trail. Twenty minutes later, we found ourselves in a farmer's front yard.

Here you'll pass through a passageway where a water tap awaits. The peaceful silence will be broken only by the barking of dogs that seem to call out, "Buon giorno!"

"So basically, we're to sneak into someone's yard, steal their water, and get ambushed by snarling Rottweilers."

"Well, we could either go all the way around, however far that is, or we could go up this hill and cut across his vineyard."

You know those inclines on, say, The Tallest Roller Coaster in the World, where the car goes clink-clink-clink-clink as it struggles to get up the track? This was the Tuscan hill version. I looked to the left, where the trail around the vineyard disappeared far into the horizon and started up the hill. Thirty sweaty, slow-motion minutes later, we reached the top. Inhibitions gone, we cut across the vineyard, helped ourselves to a few of the grapes, meandered down a few side roads, and ended up in a lovely green meadow, singing folk songs a trifle off key. Things were definitely looking up. Then:

Bonnie: "I think we're going too far east. We have to start heading north."

To the north, a dark forest ascended a steep hill beyond a stream overgrown with rose bushes. Clearly, it must be the path.

"There's a log here," Bonnie called out. "If we could throw it and position it just right, we could use it to cross the stream."

Oh, yes. That'll work. Let's calculate the exact angle at which to fling a log the length of a truck so that it forms a natural bridge over the stream. It was a Boy Scout's dream. We managed instead to cross the stream with only minor cuts and scratches, then entered a forest we nicknamed Murkwood.

> **Oh, yes. That'll work. Let's calculate the exact angle at which to fling a log the length of a truck.**

Using vines, we heaved ourselves up the hill, sliding down frequently on the slippery carpet of leaves. The BEWARE WILD BOARS sign at the forest's edge was not encouraging. I was sure the rabid creatures were waiting to pounce from behind every bush.

Finally we emerged—covered in leaves, burrs, and thin lines of blood—to find ourselves staring at an immense, rolling, plowed field of dried mud. We're not talking garden-tool-sized plowed furrows here. We're talking deep, thick, sink-into-'em, stumble-over-'em furrows. I lifted up my water bottle, hoping that somehow there'd be a few drops left, like when you find five dollars in your pocket. But it betrayed me.

Trudge, slog. Trip, sink. A dusty dew of sweat covered us. An ageless hour later, we reached the crest of the hill, to reveal … another plowed field. I was beginning to understand how Moses felt during his 40 years in the desert.

"What do you think is beyond this hill?" he'd ask his wife. "I'd say about another twenty years of desert, Mo," she'd answer, fed up. "When we get to Canaan, I'm throwing that damn *Hiking in Sinai* book into the burning bush!"

More plodding, sinking, sweating. This was not at all what we were led to expect. I know what you're thinking. *Whiner*, you're thinking. I should be grateful. I could be stuck in (a) an office, (b) a third-world country with a ruthless dictator, (c) a wheelchair, or (d) a really small hole. I know. Yet who among us wouldn't rather be in a traffic jam than in any of the above, and who hasn't complained about a traffic jam?

Trudge, slog. Trip, sink. What I wouldn't give for water.

"Look up ahead!" Bonnie exclaimed.

The crest of the hill revealed the end of the plowed fields and the familiar towers rising in the distance. We stepped onto a narrow dirt road lined with cypress trees. Up ahead, a cheerful old man stood in front of . . . a water spigot! It was a vision.

"*Acqua! Per favore!*" we choked.

"*Certo, certo!*" he beamed, filling our water bottles. We asked him in Italian if it was very far to the village. Not far at all, he told us, a somewhat puzzled expression on his face. No doubt he was wondering why two girls would want to trudge through the countryside, looking as if they'd been through a small war, when they could just sit on a hill somewhere and drink wine. We strolled down the road, chugging our water. It was that time of day when the sky has a dusky glow, when the air is cool and sweet. Laughter drifted from flower-boxed windows; cypress shadows stretched out across the path.

Back in town, Bonnie bought a bottle of red and we sat on a grassy area overlooking the countryside. "What smells so good?" she asked. We sank our hands into the wild mint beneath us, pulling up bunches and inhaling the fragrance. Then we smiled at each other, half in joy and half in frustration, because life is cruel. Just when you want to feel supremely sorry for yourself, it sends you a mint field, Chianti, and the sunlight setting aglow the towers of San Gimignano.

KERIDWEN CORNELIUS *has been lost, stranded, embarrassed, robbed and groped on several continents, yet she keeps coming back for more. Her work has appeared in* The Arizona Republic *and* The Irish Letter *and, soon,* Arizona Highways *magazine. She is at work on a novel.*

Siena

Between Naples and Memphis

abel g. peña

The hypnotic sound floated delicately into my room, charming me as only a beautiful song does, commanding me to follow as only a foreign tongue can. It was a dozen steps through the small living room to the kitchen where I found her. I'd been in Italy a little more than a week. My command of the language was negligible, and I knew she didn't speak a squeak of English. But the crests and dips of her voice carried a remarkably familiar ring, whipping my soul into a frenzy.

I know this song! I thought.

Something inside me burned, longing to join her

in song. So as she leapt again into the first refrain of "*O sole mio*," singing "*Che bella cosa!*," I did.

In English.

It's now or never...!

Slightly startled, she spun around to identify the owner of this new voice. With an unspoken understanding, we continued.

Una giornata di sole—Come hold me tight
Un'aria serena—Kiss me my darling
Dopo la tempesta—Be mine tonight

And somewhere in the gulf between Italian folk song and American oldies, Naples and Memphis...

Per l'aria fresca—To-morrow
sembra gia festa—will be too late

... we fell in love, my *nonna* and I.

Che bella cosa—It's now or never
Una giornata di sole!—My love won't wait!

The University of California had arranged for me to live with Anna in her little house just outside the walls of Siena. The agreement between us was simple: She would wash and iron my clothes for me (despite my weak protests), teach me Italian, and cook for me; and I would love her like my own *nonna*, my own grandmother.

There are two ways to say I love you in Italian.

If addressing your true love, the appropriate version is the straightforward *Ti amo*. If addressing a father, mother or other loved one, it's the more complex *Ti voglio bene*, which translates to, "I want you good." Clumsy, but definitely preferable to telling your grandma you want her bad.

Over a period of two and a half months, Anna and I became very close, and I got to know the particulars of her personality. She had a fond desire to visit Holland, and she longed to return to *bella Napoli*. She was indifferent toward Italy's most towering literary work, Dante's *Inferno* ("What the hell is this Dante saying? I can't understand him"), supportive of the war in Iraq ("Your president gave Saddam an ultimatum. Now he must follow through or appear less a man"), partial to wine and cigarettes (hardly out of the ordinary in Italy—), and a fan of Colombo reruns (—this, however, was).

We quickly fell into a comfortable schedule. Monday through Thursday, we would eat a simple biscotti and café latte breakfast together, chat it up on the odd afternoon, and then, each night, eat and drink in grand fashion with her beautiful and educated 40-year-old daughter, Cinzia, in a small 10-by-12-foot space that doubled as dining and living room.

Adorning the walls around us were framed portraits of Anna's late husband, the legendary Giorgio, or "Vittorino" to his friends and admirers (literally, "little victor").

I knew little about the horseman. Early in my stay, Anna had shown me a book that had been written about him and his horse. She took it down from a shelf in the living room, showing me its contents with great care, as well as a wariness that suggested she feared I might eat the pages if I got too close. Vittorino had emerged triumphant in Siena's biannual Palio—a terrifyingly feral horserace running the perimeter of the city's central plaza—an astounding eight times.

How Cinzia misses him, Anna had said, and oh how Cinzia loved him.

Using her daughter's name was a cheap veil, but effective nonetheless. For though Anna stared long and hard at her husband's frozen image on the wall, though her eyes were scarcely still behind the thin mist that enveloped them, she did not spill a tear.

Maybe I can read the book sometime? I said. Perhaps when you learn to read Italian a little better, she suggested, carefully closing the book and trying not to return it too quickly to its place on the shelf. Some time would pass before we spoke of Vittorino for the second and final time.

Each Friday, I took off for the weekend to visit some far-flung Italian city, from Venice to Pompeii. But one weekend, I made an 11th-hour decision with a few friends to go see Amsterdam instead. Leaving on Friday and not returning until Tuesday, it was to be the longest I had been away from Siena yet.

"So, you're leaving tomorrow," Anna said.

"I'll be back next week"

"You're going to miss school?"

"Yes, Anna."

"And where," Cinzia asked in her usual teacher-like tone, "are you going? Amsterdam?"

"Uh." Caught. "Yes," I said.

She nodded, emitting a delicate, "Ah."

"Your *professoressa* is okay with this?" Anna asked.

"Certainly."

"*Va bene!* Have a great trip!"

Hygiene and diet got tossed on that trip quicker than a tourist can yell, "Train strike!" I brought a vicious cold back with me to Siena; my body was getting even with me for all the abuse I'd put it through. However, while I was away, I made sure to remember one very important thing.

"Anna, I have something for you."

"What do you mean, you have something for me?"

I asked her to close her eyes. She eyed me shrewdly, her wrinkled chin shifting to one side and her lips parting in suspicion. This was old hat. I'd received the same reaction when trying to surprise her with a flower I'd bought one day inside the city walls.

"*Per favore, Anna! Chiude i due occhi.*" She closed her eyes. I scrutinized her face for signs of peeking.

Don't look, I said.

I'm not looking! she said, the rest of her spitfire protest too fast for me to follow.

"*Apre le mani.*"

She opened her old, soft hands, forming a cleft bowl. Gently, I rested the item in her palms.

"Open."

Her eyes opened, and fell upon a fist-sized ball of crinkled Dutch newspaper. For a long moment she puzzled at it, as if staring at a futuristic contraption. She did not look at me, and for an instant I felt an irrational surge of failure.

Then, however, she unwrapped the small package with the concentration and zeal of a little girl, and my anxiety passed.

She did not look at me, and for an instant I felt an irrational surge of failure.

....

"It's beautiful!" she exclaimed, even before she'd gotten a proper eyeful of the object.

"It says *Olanda*," I said, translating the word for Holland written on the side of the ceramic trinket. I pointed to the small, sculpted windmill. "See?"

Now she did take it all in: a small windmill standing chaperon to a little boy and girl Eskimo kissing in a colorful field of flowers.

"Beautiful."

I pointed at each figure in turn. "You see," I explained, "there's Little Abel and there's Little Anna."

She stared at the two miniature figures.

"In another lifetime," I said.

Grazie, she said. I think. I don't remember, to be honest. What I do remember is the look of recognition

She stared at her gift a bit longer, and then her eyes locked on me with a terrible suddenness. It was a sad look, an accusing look. Again, I felt an irrational surge of emotion, fear this time. Her hurt gaze spoke of betrayal, of an unexpected breach in an emotional reservoir she hadn't known, or remembered she had. And it spoke of resignation.

"Do you like it, Anna?"

Over Anna's shoulder, Vittorino's portrait peered at us with haughty disdain.

"I love it, *amore.*"

"He was a bad husband," Anna said, "but a good man."

Or perhaps it was the other way around.

One week was all I had left in Italy. Almost three months had passed since I'd gone to Holland, and almost as long since I'd moved out of Anna's house and into a place of my own. I had been all over Europe, from Sicily to England, from Spain to the Czech Republic.

Now, we were sharing an espresso at midday, back at our little table in our little house in our little living room/dining room. Anna was smoking.

Vittorino's pictures hung in three different places, one behind Anna's chair and two behind mine. Of the three, two were portraits. The one behind me had Vittorino posing in an outfit with the *nicchio,* or shells, representing the territory of the city in which

Anna now lived. The one behind Anna seemed a bit older, in which his jockey outfit sported the symbol of a rival *contrada*, or neighborhood. In each, his image was idealized as though in a Renaissance painting: the strong set of his jaw, the challenging tilt of his chin, and the fearless look in his eye as he gazed over his shoulder at the viewer—a portrayal of arrogance that invited admiration more than envy. The last painting, done in a fascinating style that seemed more retro Oriental than traditionally European, had him riding toward victory.

The conversation about Vittorino picked up where we had left off almost six months previous. She spoke disdainfully of him, his egoism, his vices and his temper. He was a man with faults, she told me, faults of a kind characteristic of men of an older time. And she had suffered the brunt of these. But the longing gaze she cast over my shoulder at the object of her scorn told another part of the story.

How long ago? I ventured to ask.

Dead three years now, she said.

She missed him, she said, it was true. "How could I not? Since I was fifteen years old, he was the only man that I ever knew."

She stared longingly at the image beside me, of an ageless, proud, unapologetic and unforgiving champion.

"A good man," she said.

❖

Some scientists have postulated that the capacity to create and understand music is the highest form of communication the human brain has attained.

Two nights before I left Italy behind, as the sound of Andrea Bocelli's rich voice coated us in waves of "*Con Te Partiro*" and, of course, "*O Sole Mio*" from a stage in Siena's central plaza, I might have agreed.

Alas, the next night, the last time I saw Anna, there was no singing. On that last day, after nearly half a year living in Italy, we simply sat together and ate, just the two of us.

"Cinzia's not here?"

"Cinzia went out to eat with a friend. She sends her love."

We rehashed subjects about which we'd spoken a hundred times, watched Italian game shows with their scantily clad women. At other times there was silence.

Tomorrow I would be gone. It was now or never.

"I will miss you, Anna."

To say I miss you in Italian is not possible. The phrase that is used instead, *Mi manchi*, gives possession of the action, of the "missing," to the person being addressed. Instead of saying you miss someone, a better translation might be, "I am lacking you."

I puffed up with pride when my *nonna* responded that she couldn't understand why, of all the students who had lived with her, she had grown so attached to this one, to me. *I don't know*, she said, shaking her head with great concern. *I don't know.*

Like a man, I ventured to give a complex answer, in inadequate Italian, to a woman three times my age, for a question that was not a question. For a second, she stared at me, this proud Tuscan woman. Longer. Her eyes glazed. Again that unflinching gaze.

Then, like a woman three times my age, she nodded sympathetically, as if she remembered having heard some similar nonsense years and years ago, once upon a time. Anna and I kissed each other good night on both cheeks, our eyes meeting one final time before she unhesitatingly shut the door.

I do not think that music is the highest form of communication. I think, rather, it is the ability to communicate without making a sound.

"I've always loved you!" my heart sang in desperation in that last moment. And in *contrapasso*, her stone eyes replied, "I've loved you longer."

ABEL G. PEÑA (*www.abelgpena.com*) *is a California-based writer best known for his extensive contributions to Lucasfilm Ltd.'s Star Wars franchise, including work for Star Wars Insider, StarWars.com, and Vader: The Ultimate Guide. When Abel isn't pretending to be an Ewok, he's working like a dog. Having seen Europe, he plans to travel to Japan and Australia to see how the other side of the world lives.*

Siena

Hostage of the Hostile Hostel

bill fink

■ ran the two miles to the hostel outside Siena, my
backpack bouncing painfully on my shoulders.
The manager had told me they had only one space
remaining. It was all I could afford in the area—I had
to get that spot.

When I arrived, panting, at the three-story brick-
and-steel building, I was dismayed to see a mob of
backpackers crowded around the front desk. Two
surly staff members were shouting at them in Italian,
grabbing crumpled piles of money, and stuffing
registration forms, one each, into the hundred cubby
holes in the wall behind them. Each nook denoted one

166 ITALY FROM A BACKPACK

available bed. As I made my way to the counter, I heard one of the clerks answer the phone.

"No! No reservations! One space only. You come now. Immediately!" He slammed down the phone.

I looked at the wall behind him; at least two dozen cubby holes were empty.

As I exchanged my money for bed #42, the clerk pointed an accusing finger at me and spouted the rules in heavily accented English: "No drinking! No food! No noise at night! Lights out at midnight! Curfew eleven-thirty—absolutely no entry after then, doors locked! Doors locked ten in morning to three in afternoon. Everyone must go. Absolutely no entry! Doors locked until seven in morning. No entry, no exit!"

Surely they wouldn't mind if I needed the rules to be altered just a bit.

This rigid set of commands seemed better suited to the countries I'd just left, famously uptight Switzerland and Germany. Italy was supposed to be the home of the sun-drenched, relaxed attitude of the Mediterranean. Surely they wouldn't mind if I needed the rules to be altered just a bit.

"*Signore, per favore*, I have to catch a bus at seven in the morning, so I need to leave a little earlier, maybe six-thirty. Hope it's not a problem."

"Impossible!"

I guessed he thought it would be impossible for me, if I left at 6:30, to walk the two miles back to town in time to make the Rome bus departure. It was nice of him to be concerned.

"No, no, six-thirty OK." I made a running motion with my arms.

He looked at me with what appeared to be pure hatred.

"Maybe six-fifteen?"

"IMMM-POSSIBLE!" He waved his raised hands vigorously, as if he were trying to keep an airplane from landing on the counter between us.

"No, really." I tried to explain myself slowly and simply. "I must catch bus. Only one morning bus. Seven in the morning. I must get to Rome tomorrow afternoon. So I must leave hostel by six-thirty."

"No. Impossible. Im-possible." He waved his hand to the side, dismissing me like a serf.

I stood there, stupefied, until anxious backpackers jostling for the hostel's "one last space" bumped me away from the counter.

I hoped it was just a linguistic misunderstanding. He must have meant that the doors were locked to keep people from entering before the desk was open. They couldn't possibly lock people *inside* the hostel, could they?

At 6 a.m., I crept down the stairs to the lobby, figuring that if I was quiet enough, I could unlock the front door and nobody would be the wiser.

But I couldn't even get to the front door. A set of interior glass doors divided the stairwell from the entrance. Not only were these doors locked, but a couch had been moved across them as a barricade. And on the couch slept a guard dog. It raised its head, starting to snarl before its eyes were even open. I fled up the stairs, hoping the dog wouldn't bark and wake up the manager—who, apparently, would throw me into some Medici-inspired torture chamber in a dungeon beneath the building.

I returned to my room, where 10 backpackers lay half-awake on rickety iron bunk beds.

"What, doors locked, really?" asked one German teen to whom I had told my problem. "It is like prison, ya?"

"Ya. And now I need to escape." I opened our second-story window and looked down to the asphalt below.

"No jumping. This I think is bad," said a pimply Danish high-schooler, sitting up in his bunk. I had teased him the night before about the high suicide rate in Denmark, and I think he still felt obligated to point out living solutions in our daily lives.

I started to strip the sheets off of my bed and knot them into a rope of sorts. The German and Dane jumped out of bed to do the same, waking their friends with their laughter.

We formed three sets of sheets into a 20-foot strand so I could lower my backpack, full of breakable souvenirs and my camera, to the pavement. I held the knotted end of another sheet and stepped out the window onto a small ledge. My backpacking escape team held the other end, anchoring against one of the bed frames.

I inched along the ledge until I could grasp a drain pipe bolted onto the side of the building. It was large enough that I was able to shimmy down the building without incident. I hopped onto the street.

The worried faces poking out my window burst into cheers until I quickly silenced them with a finger to my lips. I glanced toward the front doors, expecting them to burst open with the desk clerks and rabid dog leaping out to drag me back inside. I unknotted the sheets from my backpack and, after a couple of tries, tossed them back through the window.

It was already 6:40. I strapped on my backpack and started my jog into town, worried about missing the bus. As I hustled up the road, a few people working in the fields looked at me with alarm. I imagined their thoughts: The only people who ran in Italy were thieves and soccer players, and I wasn't wearing a jersey.

I arrived at the bus terminal, drenched in sweat, at 7:05. There wasn't a single person in the waiting area. The bus must have left! I gnashed my teeth and cursed the hostel loudly. A sleepy head poked out from behind the ticket window. "*Che?*"

"The bus, the seven o'clock Rome bus, is it gone? Can I still catch it at another station in town?"

The ticket clerk recoiled at my wide-eyed, sweaty countenance. Then he laughed.

"No, no, no, seven o'clock bus, she never come at seven." He wagged his finger. "Seven o'clock bus always come after nine." He slammed the shutter closed behind the window. I heard it click.

Reflexively, I looked for an exit, worried they had locked me inside again.

BILL FINK *was a comparative-literature major at the University of Michigan. He spent the summer after graduation hitchhiking across Europe, getting rides with everyone from cheerful soccer hooligans to grumpy prison guards. Years later, the hostel in this story still gets crappy reviews from backpackers. Bring rope.*

Siena

Art Appreciation

jessica silliman

as I enter the small room in Siena's Museo dell'Opera del Duomo, I quickly inhale. Hanging in front of me is one of the things that led me to Italy. Her gaze penetrates me and leaves me star-struck. I'm breathless.

Two years ago, on a cold, gloomy day in March, I sat in the dark with 30 other students, my eyes transfixed by slide after slide of early Renaissance art, projected on our classroom wall. With each illuminated image, my professor described how the artist had surpassed the works of those before him as he had recognized the power of his brush, and his ability to create light and shade. Flat, static folds of robes accentuated with gold triangles gradually became voluptuous, natural images, gaining space, movement and weight. Cimabue bested the Baroque artists and Giotto built on the ideas of Cimabue, but Duccio, the student of Cimabue, perfected it all. In the 14th century he was the prize of Siena, the highly acclaimed master of the Sienese School of Painting.

And now, I am standing before Duccio's majestic *Maesta*, a 13-by-7-foot panel that dwarfs me. But this painting doesn't appear to be the same one I once studied. I remembered the Madonna appearing flat, even dull. When I first saw her, she looked uncomfortable and out of place on her throne. But now she looks different: grand, dignified, vivacious.

I hear the words of my professor in my ears, her idyllic voice telling us about this work of art. *The Maesta is almost 700 years old. Completed in 1311, it is now considered one of the most important late-medieval paintings in all of Europe. Duccio is praised for the full, soft faces he gives the Virgin, and the angels and saints flanking her sides. The figures have volume, and their overlapping nature gives the piece space.*

With my own eyes, I can now see what my professor was talking about, understand the revolutionary, three-dimensional aspects of this piece. I can finally comprehend the words I regurgitated on my final test that spring quarter when this slide came shooting out of the projector. Now I can see so much more: Duccio was a master.

The Madonna sits in the center of the piece, towering over the saints, angels and prophets that accompany her. If standing, she would rise to nearly three times the height of her court, but the disproportion doesn't hinder the work. Instead, it draws in the audience and transfixes the eye upon the Virgin. She holds the Christ Child with both arms, and the little man sits peacefully upon her lap, elegantly wrapped in shimmering fabric.

My eyes always come back to meet those of the Madonna.

....

My eye wanders from the gold of Christ's cloak to the same color encircling the heads of the angels. The sparkle of the saints' ruby-red robes leads me around the painting, but my eyes always come back to meet those of the Madonna. Her vibrant royal-blue cloak, withstanding the test of time, draws appreciation from the discerning eye. Any art critic knows that blue is the most difficult tempera-paint color to create, and it deteriorates with age; therefore, this precious color is reserved for only the most sacred of subjects. The Madonna certainly qualifies.

I sit in the center of the 20-odd empty folding chairs placed beneath her. Then I realize I'm not alone. In the corner chair, an aging man, slouched with outstretched legs slightly apart, appears to be nodding off. His black boot tapping the creaking wooden floor is the only indication of life. His job is to sit and watch. He must watch people come in, stare, and leave, every day, for hours on end. As I watch him and contemplate his profession, a man scuffles in with a Rick Steves guidebook tucked under his arm, pages creased and binding bent. He walks quickly and directly to the guard. "Duccio?" he asks, either for lack of Italian or lack of time. With the nod of the guard, the man steps back, stares at the Madonna for mere seconds, then spins on his heels to exit. The guard sees my look of disgust and winks. Even though he sees her every day, he understands the power of the Virgin, her gaze and her grandeur.

This type of museum-goer bothers me. I clearly recall my art-history professor sternly warning my freshman ancient-art class never to be this type of wanderer. Even if you don't "like" it stylistically, you must take the time to absorb a work and appreciate it for what it is, or for what it has done for the art world. But I can relate to the dashing man. I was once in his shoes. As a child, I loathed being pulled through museum after museum. I'd rather have had Brussels sprouts shoved down my throat. The reason was simple: I didn't understand art. My college required students to take three sequential history courses; I settled on art history for lack of anything better. Literature was full, performing arts was uncomfortably empty, and classic history was taught by a professor with green hair.

As the lights dimmed on the first day of art lecture, and the projector whirled behind me, my apprehensions melted. I realized art was different.

Knowledge of the history, background and context was the key to appreciating it. Each painting and sculpture was created for a purpose. Looking at a painting allows anyone to travel through time.

So we sit together, the guard and I, in this shabby room, its stark, hospital-white walls and wood laminate floors completely unbefitting the Madonna. Her eyes stare directly across the room, where they land upon a panel of the same size about 30 feet away. It was once affixed to her back, as the other side of an altarpiece. That panel depicts 14 scenes of the life of Christ—the life of the blessed child she holds in her arms. Out of the corner of her eye, she may catch a glimpse of the work of another master, Pietro Lorenzetti, whose *Birth of a Virgin* clings to the wall. Though now it looks to be a futile attempt at perspective, Lorenzetti's effort was pioneering, and it inspired others to try this same monumental task.

After glancing around the room, my eyes wander once again to the Madonna. I can't help but be engulfed by the swirling colors and vibrant gold plating. I'm awed that so many years ago, Duccio—along with the clergy, government officials, and every last Sienese citizen—carried this work, in procession with glowing candles, from his studio to the high altar of the Duomo. Shops closed so that everyone could take part in the celebration streaming from the Campo. They walked the path I had taken today, this same trail of history, down Via di Citta and up Via del Capitano, to the Duomo, this museum most pass by, in this city, this Italy. As I leave the room, taking one last look at the Madonna, I turn to the guard with an approving nod and say, *"Grazie."*

A JUNIOR at Santa Clara University, Jessica Silliman is an aspiring investigative journalist majoring in communication, with minors in business and art history. Before her four-month study abroad in Perugia, Italy, she spent the summer in Ghana, West Africa, working for a political newspaper. She now has the itch to travel the world and, if all goes well, do some writing along the way.

Siena

Layering

danielle mutarelli

during my junior year in college, I set out to study abroad in the Mother Land—Italy. Unfortunately, my luggage did not make the trip with me. Thus, I arrived in Italy exactly as my great-grandfather had arrived in America, with nothing more than the clothes on my back.

Ten days later, my luggage and I were reunited; I was elated. For more than a week, I had been obsessing about a clean pair of jeans. But when I tore into my bags, I found that most of my lightly colored clothes were stained. Somewhere along its journey, my luggage apparently had been left sitting in a puddle of water that had seeped into most of what I'd packed.

Siena's winters are damp and raw, and I hadn't foreseen that. Everything I had packed was lightweight, so I had to layer stained shirt upon stained shirt in order to keep warm. In a country so famous for its fashion and good taste, I looked like a refugee.

In December, weeks before my course began, I met with the program director in his office on campus. It was a gray day, and he was in a melancholy mood. He asked me why I wanted to come to Italy. I thought the answer was obvious: because it was Italy.

He gazed out the window and said, "There isn't a lot to do in Siena. It can be boring; it gets lonely." At the time I thought it was an odd thing to say. I imagined my experience to be a scene out of *La Dolce Vita*, or a snapshot from Carnevale. As it turned out, I just wished somebody had told me to pack a sweater.

I lived with seven girls in a two-bedroom apartment in the old section of Siena, just a block away from Piazza del Campo. The apartment was hundreds of years old, with high ceilings, crown molding and tall, green-shuttered windows that looked out on Sant'Agostino. The hall and entryway floors were tiled in black and white marble; what little furniture we had was antique and gothic-looking. It was gorgeous and we were all impressed, until we realized the apartment had no heat. We kept our coats on at all times. At night, we huddled in our beds and spoke in puffs of fog. I wanted another blanket. I craved a warm body. One night, we woke to discover that our jar of Nutella had frozen.

Fortunately, soon after our arrival, we discovered the city's open-air market, a sea of stalls spread between the Fortress and Piazza Gramsci. Frigid foreigner that I was, I descended upon it, loaded myself with myriad merino-wool sweaters, and bought as many as I could afford, which for a student living abroad amounted to three. I wore them all at once.

As I didn't speak the language, I was enrolled in an intensive Italian course. It was filled with students from all around the world, and taught in an immersion method where the instructor speaks only Italian. In theory, this sounds fast and effective, but in my case, it resulted only in my neither understanding what the instructor said to me, nor being able to repeat what I was asked back to her.

Apparently I was not alone in wading through these gulfs of incomprehension. In class one day, our teacher unleashed us upon each other, pairing us up and instructing us to conduct a conversation in Italian. I was under the impression that I'd asked my partner what he'd like to be when he grew up. He looked me square in the eye and, looking quite pleased with himself, said, "Blue."

I found that this system was flawed.

I was forced to rely on my trusty English-Italian dictionary, which I carried with me at all times. It proved to be a dangerous tool in the hands of a novice such as myself. One night, my roommates and I were invited to a party hosted by some of the local university students.

I stood in a corner with an unlit cigarette in one hand and the dictionary in the other, flipping through pages to find the verb for "to light," *accendere*. But in my zealousness to communicate, I failed to notice that this verb also means "to turn on." I tapped the shoulder of the fellow beside me and asked in Italian, "Can you turn me on?"

He smiled and said, "*Sì.*"

After months of study, my fellow classmates saw my case as hopeless and voted me The Person Least Likely to Ever Speak Italian. My problem was that I had previously studied French, Spanish, German and Portuguese. I thought that this would work in my favor, but it did not. I was a walking Tower of Babel. I knew too many words in too many languages. Some stood out to me as unique to their own specific language, whereas others floated around in my head with the potential, if spoken with an Italian accent, to *become* Italian words. Of course, the accent always sounded convincing in my head, but spoken out loud, it sounded more like a bad John Wayne impersonation. People could neither understand me nor resist the urge to laugh.

After class, I would take solitary hikes outside the city's medieval walls, in the Tuscan hills, amidst the cypress trees, past the vineyards and farmhouses. Every view looked like a postcard. I saw sights so breathtaking, they made me cry.

Somehow in this storybook land, I'd imagined that it would be a breeze to find romance, in Venice and Rome, Assisi and Capri, Milan, Florence, Elba, all such beautiful locations filled with such handsome men. Between indulging in creamy *cannoli* and frothy cappuccinos, I thought it would be a snap to lose my heart. I envisioned myself returning home having had as many affairs as I had photos. But in Italy, I was robbed of my gift of gab and bereft of my pick-up lines. I never dreamed I'd be so lonely.

On Sundays, I attended Mass at the magnificent Duomo cathedral, the jewel in the crown of Sienese architecture. Constructed in the 13th century by leading artists of the day, its interior pillars, striped in black and white, support a vaulted ceiling painted a deep blue and dotted with gold stars. It is an awe-inspiring structure. I admit that I went there to check out guys.

> **But in Italy, I was robbed of my gift of gab and bereft of my pick-up lines. I never dreamed I'd be so lonely.**

It was not until late April, when the temperatures rose, the flowers bloomed, and I was able to peel off two of my five layers, that I met Massimo. I met him in Piazza del Campo, where twice a year the Palio, Tuscany's most famous festival, is held. Men would race horses bareback, their hands gripping the manes in a festival of fear and exhilaration, terror and passion. I could never quite envision this square as it would look transformed for the Palio, the ground covered in sand, mattresses lining the walls of the sharpest turns, the crush of bodies crowding in from all directions, shouting. But least of all could I see the horses; wild horses without saddles, pawing at the ground, nostrils flaring, barely contained.

I looked across the square and caught sight of Massimo's striking green eyes, his mouth curling into a smile. He came over, sat down beside me, and spoke to me in the melodious language I will always adore but hold no hope of ever understanding. Fortunately, my roommate was fluent, and she graciously leaned in and translated.

He told me that he was from Sicily and I said that I'd never been there. He insisted that I go, that it was a world unto itself. He told me of ancient ruins and quaint villages. I was turned on by his descriptions of summer nights when it is so hot they sleep outside, on the beaches, under the stars, sometimes naked with nothing more than a thin sheet covering them, the warm Sirocco winds blowing up from Africa as they swim beneath the moonlight. I told him I was from Cape Cod, where Jaws was filmed.

In a bar one night, a friend told me a joke in English. I laughed so hard I had to cover my mouth. Massimo looked at me and shook his head sadly. My roommate translated his words as, "I can never make you laugh. You wouldn't understand the joke." I replied, "That's okay. I'm blond. I never understand the joke but I laugh anyway." He smiled and wrapped an arm around me.

Yet I knew he was right; it wouldn't work.

Communication was too important to both of us. And so, days later we parted company, in the same spot we had met—in the Campo at sunset. It was poetic and sad, and the closest I came to an Italian fling.

Weeks later, I was strolling along during the evening *passageita*, the city's nightly promenade. It was warm, and I was finally walking as I had envisioned myself in Italy—wearing a sundress and sandals, with my last layer tied around my waist. Some Americans stopped me for directions to a hostel, and then asked if I knew of any good bars. I walked them to their hostel, and then took them to our favorite haunt. Then I drew on their map and made copious notes of places to visit in and around Siena. I unloaded on them every scrap of information I'd collected in my months there. I was thrilled to share with them, flushed with excitement at knowing a place so far from home so intimately.

Walking home from the bar that night, I glowed like the rose-colored bricks of the city. Somewhere along the way, Siena had ceased to feel so cold and lonely to me. Halfway down my street, I stopped and looked back. The voices carried toward me from the Campo. Echoing off the walls, animated, they hugged me with inexplicable warmth.

DANIELLE MUTARELLI *is a freelance writer living in New Hampshire. She has recently renewed her passport (with a halfway decent photo—hurray!) and dreams of returning to Italy during the summer months, or with warm clothing.*

CARTOLINA POSTALE

LE PIÙ BELLE TERME DEL MONDO
SALSOMAGGIORE
PERIODO DI CURA
MARZO — NOVEMBRE

Venice is like eating
an entire box of
chocolate liqueurs
at one go.
- Truman Capote

Venezia
& Il Nord

Lake
Maggiorre
Nanno·
·Venezia

Italy

Venice

Forgotten Golashes

megan michelson

i was standing in a pool of water up to my ankles when it dawned on me: I love Venice. It took only a couple of hours in this deliriously romantic city. I had fallen hard, like a schoolgirl feeling her first playground crush. A sip of local red wine rivaled the sweetness of my first kiss; the sound of water in the canals was like a lover's whisper in my ear. The only thing dampening my infatuation: Venice often floods in November, and I had forgotten to pack my galoshes.

During a year studying abroad in England, I had traveled extensively. I'd buy cheap tickets to Munich or Geneva, and spend long weekends wandering aimlessly through museums and cafés. When a friend asked me to join him in Italy for a few days, I jumped at the chance. I'd never seen the country before, and I was in the mood for a change of pace from England's dreary, wet days. And part of me secretly hoped that I might stumble into a Romeo-and-Juliet kind of Italian love affair. I never would have guessed that I would fall for a place instead.

I felt a rush to navigate our way into the city, catch a water bus, find a hostel, and fall in love before the break of dawn.

Our plane was delayed out of London, so my friend Dave and I didn't land at Venice's Marco Polo airport until nearly midnight. In the darkness of the wee hours, I felt a rush to navigate our way into the city, catch a water bus, find a hostel, and fall in love before the break of dawn.

The water-bus station looked like something out of a 1980s science-fiction film. Faint bulbs cast glowing shadows over the tired faces of the Italian travelers and foreign tourists, who stood waiting on long, wooden platforms stretched over black waters. After some deliberation, we hopped aboard the Numero Cinque boat. Most of the weary passengers took seats, but Dave and I stood, large backpacks protruding behind us as we looked over the stern into the crashing wake. We skimmed by long rows of colorful, stone buildings, elaborately decorated with tall columns and graceful arches. Their ornateness contrasted with the perfect simplicity of our lives at that moment. The city slept soundly, and the only audible noises were the boat's engine and the rushing water behind us. Dave and I were quiet, too.

The Adriatic sea air felt warm and sticky, even though it was November, almost Thanksgiving back home in the States. My cheeks flushed and my body tingled with the excitement of a new, exotic place. After several stops, we hastily disembarked in the center of the city, at the Piazza San Marco station. It was one o'clock in the morning, and we had no idea where we would sleep. If all else failed, we would buy a bottle of wine and pass the hours until daylight talking at the foot of the famous basilica in the center of the square.

There was just one problem: The entire *piazza* was under two feet of water. Long, wooden planks had been constructed above it to serve as walkways for pedestrians. The next day, Piazza San Marco would be inundated with hordes of tourists, backpackers and honeymooners. But tonight, it belonged to us. It was like a remote lake, surrounded not by mountains and moonlight but by cathedrals, antique shops and street lamps. Off in a corner, one dimly lighted place, the Ristorante Alla Borsa, still served a few straggling customers. It was the only source of noise in the quiet *piazza*. We walked carefully along the planks and hesitantly peeked inside its door, concerned that we may be interrupting a private dinner for two. Much to our surprise, we were greeted warmly.

"*Ciao! Benvenuto! Vorreste mangiare?*" said a man

wearing a dark, expensive suit, with hair greased back in waves on his head. We thought he may have been the owner.

"Um...do you speak English?" Dave mumbled, embarrassed.

I stepped in, assuming the usual role of lost American youth seeking guidance. "We're looking for a hostel. A place to sleep? Can you help?"

The man smelled of cigarettes and designer cologne, and his tanned skin and dark, olive-colored eyes looked as though they could capture the heart of any woman he wanted. In flawless English, he directed us to Appa Bandiera e Moro, a guesthouse close to San Marco. Before we left, we bought a bottle of his cheapest red wine with the euros we had saved on our discount flight to Italy.

We walked outside, meandering through dark alleyways, savoring the silence and taking in every inch, every detail of the ancient, flooded city—the bakery on the corner, with water seeping in through the doorway; the rainbow flags hung in windows declaring "pace" for all; the exquisite Venetian masks displayed through dirty storefront windows. We gazed like people seeing the bodies of their lovers for the first time.

For a moment, we stopped in an alleyway over-looking a canal. I was too overwhelmed by the sights to notice that the water had drenched my socks and the only pair of shoes I had packed for the weekend. At first, I felt a stab of sadness. Venice looked exactly as I had imagined it—open squares and narrow alleys providing private spaces for stolen kisses and fleeting lust—but I knew my trip here wouldn't involve those rare moments of passion. Nobody would say *"Ti amo"* to me and mean it. In the end, though, it didn't matter. I had fallen in love with the city itself.

MEGAN MICHELSON *is an assitant editor at Outside magazine and an avid traveler. She grew up hiking, biking, skiing and writing in the Sierra Nevada foothills of California. She can also be found, occasionally, in exotic European destinations, up to her ankles in adventure.*

Venice

Sleeping Like a Queen

caitlyn clauson

i was living in Rome for four weeks, taking Scandinavian studies—not the most logical combination. But when I heard about the study-abroad program, I figured: I like Europe. I'm Scandinavian. I could get school credit. Why not?

One weekend, some friends and I decided to head up to Venice on a whim. We had a simple plan: Depart from Rome on Friday, spend a couple of days exploring Venice, and return Sunday night in time for class the following day. After a few failed attempts from Rome to reserve a room in Venice, we added that to our list of things to do upon our evening arrival. In our naïve minds, not only would we successfully secure a decent hostel, but we would actually be able to find it in the dark.

The train took longer than expected, dropping us in Venice around eleven o'clock at night. Crammed into a grungy phone booth at the edge of the train station, three friends and I desperately called every hostel, *pensione* and hotel listed in our motley collection of travel guides. We broke the cardinal rule of budget traveling and considered paying full price for a room. Even at 400 euros a night, we failed to find a single vacancy. We soon discovered that both the Venetian Architectural Festival and the Venetian Film Festival were slated for this September weekend, and well-prepared—less spontaneous—travelers had claimed all of the rooms. After two hours of pleading with hotel managers, we decided to salvage what was left of our Friday night and rethink our plans.

We figured this was fate's way of encouraging us to make the most of the Venetian nightlife. We'd live *la dolce vita* for a few hours, and, after that died down, we'd wander over to Piazza San Marco and crash on some benches. To our surprise and disappointment, everything shut down at midnight.

Feeling somewhat jaded, we simply started to walk. And true to the curse of all virgin travelers in Venice, we got lost. Little did we know that a nighttime arrival in Venice, with its disorienting labyrinth of islands and alleyways, essentially guarantees an unsolicited tour of the city. Even those with the keenest sense of direction are bound to get lost. Hope toyed with us at every turn. Every alleyway led to a bridge that led to a corridor that looped back to our starting point. Finally we reached Piazza San Marco, where we spotted an enticing set of benches directly underneath the Doge's Palace.

Exhausted and bordering on delirious, we were desperate. Even the cockroaches squirming around nearby couldn't dissuade us from curling up on the benches. We wrapped ourselves up in hostelling sheets, prayed that the square wouldn't flood, and took turns sleeping. Despite the obvious drawbacks, it was a beautiful location. Off in the distance, the water lapped against gondolas; the bell tower, cathedral and palace loomed above.

> **We wrapped ourselves up in hostelling sheets, prayed that the square wouldn't flood, and took turns sleeping.**

Although an ideal backdrop, it provided a less-than-ideal night's sleep. Braving the cold with our thin sheets, we fended off lively bands of drunken teenagers who didn't exactly appreciate our presence. And their interruptions paled in comparison with the wrath of hotel owners, who brought out their brooms to brush us aside.

At 5 in the morning, we awoke, dry and alive. While all the wise tourists slept peacefully in their beds, we—albeit a dirty, smelly, sleep-deprived quartet— experienced the most brilliant of sunrises. Warm streams of crimson, orange and yellow crowned the tops of buildings, as shopkeepers swept the sun-kissed cobblestones in the foreground.

We wandered around the city that morning, thankful to have experienced what we did, and by some form of luck, we found a room for the next night. When our friends back in Rome asked about our weekend in Venice, we simply said that we slept like kings and queens, beneath a palace.

CAITLYN CLAUSON *is a Seattle native living in Ann Arbor, Michigan. As an undergraduate, Caitlyn spent one month at the University of Washington's Rome Center, where she studied Scandinavian connections to Rome. The experience prompted her to spend part of her senior year living and interning in London. She's now a graduate student at the University of Michigan in urban planning and design, studying the likes of Venice.*

Venice

Pursuit in the Piazza

brent fattore

many people say that Venice is the most romantic city in the world. Gondoliers serenade amorous couples on endless canals winding through Italy's best Romance architecture; the isle of Murano supplies glass of unmatched beauty in all shapes, colors and sizes; and every sunset sparkles off the waters in hypnotizing oranges and crimsons. But that wasn't the Venice I came to know in my short stay there.

My day started, as do so many other backpacking-through-Europe days, with a hunk of hard bread for breakfast. Then I went wandering through the streets and back alleys, emerging at Piazza San Marco for the first time. It took my breath away. So did the line for Doge's Palace. I left, scoped out all that St. Mark's Basilica had to offer, then came back to Piazza San Marco—and found that the line for Doge's Palace was even longer. That's when Rick Steves came to the rescue: Walk to the little-known Correr Museum, his guidebook said, and buy the museum pass. That would let me bypass the Doge's Palace line.

I could not justify buying the pass without walking around the Correr. I was one of the few people there, and the echoes of my footsteps on the old wooden floors were spooky. I entered a room full of marble busts. If you have seen one marble bust, you have seen them all, but on one, I noticed a nose job. The nose looked like it had been glued back on. As I leaned in closer to examine it, my ears started ringing. I had set off the alarm! Recalling horror stories of prison conditions in Italy, I scanned the room for cameras. Calmly, I started to walk back the way I came. Down the hall, I saw a woman in uniform. I thought, I can get by her and bounce for the exit. Then I saw her partner. He looked really big.

Now I was scared, so I turned around and noticed an emergency-exit door roped off in the far corner. Adrenaline pumping, I made a break for it (thank God I wore my shoes instead of flip-flops), ran down two flights of stairs, and burst through the door at the bottom. It opened right onto a street behind Piazza San

Marco. I took a couple of quick lefts and found myself staring at St. Mark's Basilica, where the crowd had thinned dramatically. I had heard footsteps running down the museum stairs after me, so I kept moving, jogging through the square, upsetting a lot of pigeons. I took another left to get out of the square and came up short right in front of a glass shop. Three cops were hanging out there. I slowed to a walk so as not to look suspicious, said *"Buon giorno,"* and walked around a few more corners.

Eventually, I stopped at a *gelateria* to catch my breath. Gelato was one of my favorite things in Italy—today especially, as the beautiful girl behind the counter was practicing her English on me. I ordered a cone and sat down to enjoy it, thinking about my narrow escape. Suddenly, I stopped licking. The Correr makes visitors check their bags, and my day bag and camera were still there. This posed a bit of a problem: How to get my stuff back without re-entering the museum? While I pondered this dilemma, an Australian couple appeared, disappointed about the long line at Doge's Palace. Thinking quickly, I told them about the trick of buying a pass at the Correr—conveniently leaving out the fact that I was now a fugitive. I showed them my pass and told them I was on my way to the palace as well.

"One small favor to ask, in exchange for this

This posed a bit of a problem: How to get my stuff back without re-entering the museum?

information," I said. "I left the museum without getting my bag." I showed them my check tag, and told them that the guards did not speak English and would not let me back in without buying another pass. "Would you mind getting my bag while you're there?"

They were hesitant, so I told them I would buy their gelato, too, and be here waiting if there was any problem. Ten minutes later, they were back with my bag, and I bought their gelato. We walked through Doge's Palace together—and I didn't touch anything.

BRENT FATTORE *spent a month backpacking around Europe and began planning future trips the day he returned. Since graduating from the University of Washington, Brent has held a variety of jobs, including selling software, coaching college baseball, and helping to publish national bestseller "Joy at Work."*

Lake Maggiore

Isla Bella, Solo

joanne flynn

"**a**ndiamo! Andiamo!"
I did not speak much Italian, but I knew that phrase: *Let's go!* I was simply trying to take photos of the islands our ferry passed on its way to Isla Bella, our destination across Lake Maggiore. The problem was that I kept finding myself in the middle of a stream of people boarding and leaving, shouting and pushing past me at each stop.

"*Scusi, scusi, fotografia,*" I pleaded as I pointed to my camera, but it was no use. They repeatedly sandwiched me like a piece of mozzarella between two slices of Italian bread. People getting on pushed me toward the back wall. People getting off pushed me toward the outside ramp. Most of my pictures turned out to be of the backs of people's heads as they pushed me out of the way.

My decision to come here seemed very simple, when I thought back on it. I was in the last month of a six-month backpacking trip around the world with my boyfriend, Ira. The first five months we would travel together; the last month, Ira would head home and I would travel alone. After spending every waking and sleeping moment with that special someone for so long, I had become used to sharing daily experiences and routines. I was not sure how I was going to get through the last month in a foreign country without him. However, I reminded myself that I was a strong, independent-minded woman, and I was determined to make it alone.

Ira left from Milan in the middle of the summer. The heat was melting my gelato faster than I could eat it. I decided it was time get out of the city and head to the cooler lake areas up north. With several to choose from, I wanted a recommendation.

"Which lake is the best?" I asked an Elvira-looking woman at the front desk of my hostel.

"Ahh, Lake Maggiore is the most breathtaking of all the lakes in Italy, but Lake Como is where George Clooney lives," she replied with a dreamy look, batting her lashes as if George Clooney stood in front of her.

I decided that a George Clooney sighting at Lake Como was probably quite rare, so I packed my backpack and boarded the next train to Lake Maggiore. In the middle of the summer in Italy, it seemed that everyone had the same idea. The train was crowded with families from Milan trying to escape the heat. The overhead rack was packed with Louis Vuitton wheelie bags, so I had to sit my backpack on my lap. The air conditioning blew only warm air. In this unbearable heat, I tried to concentrate on the view of the Italian countryside, its rolling, forested hills with towns and homes perched high among the trees. Although I was surrounded by people, I felt alone. Plugged into my iPod, I played No Doubt's "I'm Just a Girl in the World" to help combat my loneliness.

After being cramped for hours in the heated car of the train, I was ready to enjoy fresh mountain air when we arrived at Stressa on Lake Maggiore. But the air was dead still. It looked like the only place to get a good breeze was aboard one of the many ferries heading out to the islands on the lake. So I stopped by the tourist office for a look at the schedule.

But choosing a destination and deciphering the ferry schedule seemed as complicated as understanding traffic flow in Rome. Everyone in the office was busy helping customers, smoking a cigarette or sipping an afternoon espresso. Waiting for help looked like it would take as long as Michelangelo painting the Sistine Chapel. I decided to buy a ticket for whichever ferry left next, and let fate lead me. Fate chose an island filled with gardens, grottos and peacocks—Isla Bella.

As I lugged my backpack down the ramp and onto the ferry, I planned to sit on the upper deck and feel the delicious breeze flow through my hair. The first breath of fresh air caught me as I crossed the gangway over the water to board. I took this deep into my lungs and headed inside, feeling a little more confident as a solo female traveler.

My first priority was to find the door to the outside deck, where I could take in the air. But there was no "outside" on this boat. It was completely enclosed by glass—and not clean, clear glass, but glass that looked as if it was frosted to prevent people from seeing out. On closer inspection, I realized that the "frosting" was dirt. I could not believe I had left the heat of Milan to get on a fully enclosed submarine above water.

Disappointed, I settled into a seat and pressed my face against the hard glass, trying to see something, anything. On its way to Isla Bella, the ferry stopped at several towns, transferring bustling passengers at each stop. Each time the door opened to let people on or off, I made my move to get by the door, get a breeze and snap a few photographs.

This is where the shouting began. *"Andiamo! Andiamo!"*

But I was determined to get some air. After the first few push-and-shove stops, I noticed the ferryboat captain, a very stern and weathered-looking man, staring at me in disbelief. I knew from my travels that many countries placed restrictions on photographs of train stations, airports and other modes of transport. I wondered if the Italian ferries had similar laws that I was breaking right in front of the captain.

No sooner had I finished my thought than he marched over to me, yelled something in rapid-fire Italian I could not understand, and gestured for me to follow him. Oh no, this is not good, I thought. My first day alone and I am going to get arrested! My next thought was to make a break for it—I could run off the ramp and be free. The captain would never be able to catch me. Except that I'd be running with my backpack; it would be pretty easy for him to catch us both.

Oh no, this is not good, I thought. My first day alone and I am going to get arrested!

Resigned to whatever was coming, I followed the captain, head bowed. Passengers in their seats stared at us as we passed. He turned the corner and opened a Hobbit-sized door, which led to steps so small I wondered how a Hobbit could fit on them, never mind the captain. At the top of the steps, I realized we were now at the bridge. He pointed toward the open door and made a "click-click" gesture with his hands.

"*Fotografia!*" he exclaimed, as he pointed again to the small deck outside. Then I understood that he wasn't bringing me up to put me in the brig, but to let me take photos from the only place on the ferry with an open door.

I walked to the ledge and breathed in the clean air. I smiled and felt the breeze blow through my hair. "*Scusi, senorina,*" said the captain and his second officer, as they joined me on the deck. Without the barrier of the frosted glass, I was able to see the clear water, the hillside homes, and the majestic mountains. Off to the left, we saw islands sprinkled throughout the lake.

There on the bridge, the captain's demeanor was more that of a proud father's. He looked out over the mountains, the water and the boats, and said, "*Bellisimo, no?*" I agreed, "Beautiful." He made the "click-click" motion again, and I understood that he was allowing me to take a picture with him. His second officer took the camera, and I stood next to the proud captain. He took off his captain's hat and let me wear it for the photo.

The man at the wheel called us. We moved toward him inside, and I thought he wanted his picture taken, too. But, no! He wanted me to steer the ferry. He got up from his seat and gave me control of the helm. As I put my hands on the wheel and started guiding the ferry, I reflected that being "just a girl in the world" could make for some wonderful possibilities. Still wearing the captain's hat, I piloted the ferry across the lake, keeping an eye out for George Clooney.

JOANNE FLYNN *took a break from corporate America to take a backpacking trip around the world. She has no regrets over this decision. Joanne is on the board of the nonprofit organization Women Who Write. She lives in New York City.*

Milan

High Heels From Hell

reine dugas bouton

as I packed my bag for Italy, I thought that, for just one night, I would depart from my typical bummy, grungy hostel-girl mode and give myself a "fancy" night. Just once on the trip, I was determined not to look like a tourist. I knew this was not sensible, and it would take up valuable space in my backpack, but I didn't care—I tucked in an elegant outfit, including high heels.

Every other time I'd gone to Italy, I had stared with envy at the stunning Italian women, wearing their sophisticated cashmere sweaters, scarves tossed casually around their long necks, walking confidently on dramatic high heels. Could I pull that off? Could I look like an Italian? Could I fit in?

I'd bought a single outfit at Macy's: skirt, sweater, and tan and black leather pumps that I'd fallen in love with. Together, they looked stylish and, above all, Italian. I felt comfortable in this fetching ensemble as I twirled in front of my mirror at home. And I began to feel that I might just pass for someone from Rome or Milan, rather than from Metairie, Louisiana. Yes, I thought, this will work.

When I arrived at my hotel in Milan, I put on the fancy clothes, shook my hair out of its ponytail, wrapped a long, silky scarf against my neck, slid my feet into the shoes, and finished with a tiny pillbox purse clutched in my hand. It felt good to leave my backpack behind. When I stepped out to stroll down the street, my hair blowing in the breeze, it was everything I'd imagined.

There was only one problem: cobblestone streets.

For about five minutes, I strolled with the tune of "Pretty Woman" floating in my head. Then, my heel caught in a groove between the stones, and I went flying. I fell hard, fancy ensemble and all, wrenching my wrist and ankle, briefly flashing Milan as my skirt flared on my way down.

"Aaaargh! Damn it to hell!" I shouted, no longer pretending to be Italian, now clearly an American of the worst sort. I hastily adjusted my skirt with scraped, bleeding hands, then scooted gracelessly toward my shoe, now stuck upright in the street, mocking me.

"Traitor," I muttered as I yanked the pump free. No one stopped to see if I was all right; they merely bustled on by, with an occasional *"permesso"* to move past me.

Fortunately, I was only a few blocks from my hotel, so I hobbled back in my bare feet, heaving my $60 pumps into the nearest trash can. I must have looked a sight—a limping, frustrated tourist, scarf dragging the ground behind her, scuffed knees and hands, shoeless. Very un-Italian.

After a long soak in the tub, and the rationalization that Italian women have walked in high heels on bumpy streets since they were teenagers, I accepted the fact that I had set my standards too high. I didn't have the history to make such a bold attempt. What was I thinking? I wore heels at home only when I went to weddings.

> **I might have had the ensemble right, but I didn't have the attitude.**

As I thought more about it, I suspect I probably looked like a girl playing dress-up in her mother's clothes. I might have had the ensemble right, but I didn't have the attitude. I didn't fit in at all—and it wasn't the clumsy fall that was the dead giveaway.

All the times I'd sat in a *piazza*, watching Italian women go by, I had thought their style was defined by their clothes. Now I realized that what makes these women so alluring is their attitude; their graceful walk; the seductive flip of their thick, curly hair; the hidden look in their large brown eyes.

All of which I didn't have.

So the next morning, I leaned over—gingerly—to grab my pack. Got out jeans and a T-shirt. I put on my sneakers, feeling a little embarrassed, and decided to stop trying to be something I was not. After all, I was really a girl—an American girl—trekking through Italy on a shoestring budget.

REINE DUGAS BOUTON *teaches English at Southeastern Louisiana University. She is writing a critical book on contemporary travel writing about Italy, "In Search of La Dolce Vita." In addition to traveling to Italy as often as possible with her family, she has taken study-abroad groups to Tuscany for the past two summers. Daring or just plain crazy? She hasn't yet decided.*

Nanno

Finding
Signora Bacca

charlie usher

When I went to Europe, my grandmother gave
me an address. It belonged to her cousin,
Mary Bacca, whom my grandmother had never met,
but with whom she had exchanged letters for years
through a mutual friend in Indiana, who had translated
my grandmother's English to Italian, and Mary's Italian
to English.

My grandmother was born in America, but much
of her family (including her mother, whose maiden
name, Recla, was given to me as a middle name) had
emigrated from the northeastern corner of Italy. There,
they had lived in the same small cluster of villages

outside of Trento as their relatives, the Baccas. So, in the last week of my trip to Europe, on my way from Edinburgh to Rome, armed with only a rudimentary grasp of Italian and an address scribbled on a piece of scrap paper, I set out to find my last living relative in Europe.

The address was in a village called Nanno. To get there, I had to take a small regional train from Trento to Cles, then board a bus that snaked along mountainside roads before dropping me off in the village's center. Nanno was a ghost town. Every shop that I could see was closed, and there wasn't another person in sight. Granted, I had arrived in the middle of the afternoon siesta, but the absolute lack of people or sound, any sign of life at all, was unsettling. The village itself was quite pretty, but more than that, it was tiny—there couldn't have been more than 500 people living there. All around it, rising straight up from the valleys, were the Dolomites, jagged and craggy and slightly pink in the afternoon sun.

I pulled the address out of my pocket and looked around the bus stop for a village map, but there was nothing except a bulletin board posting local notices and Mass times. I hoisted my backpack onto my shoulders and started walking, thinking that, in a town this small, I'd either run into someone who could direct me or simply stumble upon the house. After a couple of minutes, I spotted a middle-aged man sitting in his driveway, but as I got closer his dog started to bark, and

I decided to keep going. Within a minute, though, I had literally reached the edge of town. The road kept going, but stretched out in front of me were acres and acres of apple orchards full of trees just beginning to bear fruit. I turned around. The dog was no longer barking, so I walked up to the man sitting in his driveway.

"*Scusi*," I said in Italian, "but do you know where this address is?" The man in the driveway stood up and took the address from me. "Oh, Mary! You're looking for Mary!"

"Yes. She's my grandmother's cousin and I'm trying to find her because I want to meet her."

"Ah, *fantastico!*" And before I knew quite what was going on, he was waving over his next-door neighbor. "Enrico, this kid's looking for Mary. He's ... what did you say you were?"

"She's my grandmother's cousin," I said.

"She's his grandmother's cousin."

"She's your grandmother's cousin?!" replied Enrico. "*Fantastico!* Come on, I'll drive you there."

Enrico took me over to his truck. I threw my backpack in the bed and jumped up in front with him. Signora Bacca's house ended up being three blocks away, and the sheer pointlessness of driving there made me appreciate Enrico's generosity even more. The two of us walked up to the front steps and Enrico rang the doorbell. There was no answer. He rang once more; again, no answer. I was just about to leave when the door opened.

Signora Bacca was short and plump, with round cheeks, dark brown eyes, and a head of wavy gray hair. She wore a long house skirt, a loose-fitting blouse and burgundy slippers. She looked almost exactly as I had pictured her. She also looked very confused. I imagined that Nanno hadn't seen a backpacker in years, if ever, and to have a young, dirty kid wearing a camping bag and three-day old beard show up on her doorstep must have been the last thing she was expecting.

Signora Bacca reached up and literally pinched my cheeks. She then reached down and took hold of my hand.

....

I introduced myself. "*Mi chiamo* Charlie. My grandmother Jean is your cousin." My Italian was good enough that I could say that much flawlessly, but still Signora Bacca looked utterly baffled. She turned to Enrico for help. He explained what was going on and suddenly her face was radiant. "Gina!" she said.

"*Sì, sì*, Jean Mlynarek. She's my grandmother." Signora Bacca reached up and literally pinched my cheeks. She then reached down and took hold of my hand before leading me inside. I thanked Enrico again and followed Signora Bacca into her house.

Her home was large for an old woman living alone. It was packed to the gills with photos of relatives, kitschy knickknacks, and religious memorabilia. She pointed me into a spare bedroom and then pulled me into the kitchen, asking me if I was hungry. Without waiting for an answer, she began to boil a pot of water on the stove.

While we waited for it to heat, Signora Bacca sat me down at the kitchen table and pulled out several volumes of photo albums. I grabbed the pictures I had been carrying with me in a Ziploc bag and showed her my family and friends. She showed me her relatives and old photos of my family at Christmas that my grandmother had sent her. We flipped through the albums together while I ate, and she let me ask her questions about her life.

My Italian was rusty from two months of disuse, and, exhausted from three days of nonstop travel, it was difficult to understand everything that she said. From what I could gather, her cat's name was Bidi, she'd never been married, and she'd worked for most of her life helping her father in the region's apple orchards. She'd been born in a nearby town and immigrated to the United States, but returned soon after to attend to her dying mother. And then she just stayed. When I asked her if she'd had a husband, she told me she'd never had time to get married. It seemed sad, thinking of her alone in this big house, in this speck of a town, and I suddenly had an uncharacteristic urge to ask her if she'd ever been in love. But it seemed too strange or rude a question to ask a woman I'd met an hour ago. Besides, she seemed happy.

When I finished eating, Signora Bacca led me outside and walked me to the main *piazza* to show me the village church. At the door she commented on something, causing me to remark that, unlike the rest of my family, I wasn't Catholic. She was a little taken aback. "But you believe in God," she pressed.

"I don't know," I replied. "Not really."

When Signora Bacca heard this, she looked more than a little incredulous, but she composed herself quickly, patted me on the shoulder, and muttered something that sounded like, "Well, you still have time to figure it out."

We walked into the nave. The church was only about 20 years old, and its simplicity matched that of its pastor, an elderly man in gold wire-rimmed glasses. Signora Bacca introduced us and then began showing me around the altar and the sacristy like she owned the place. I kept looking back at the priest to see if he minded any of this, but he was fixated on his Bible. Apparently he did not. Signora Bacca pointed out and described the numerous saints depicted in statues and stained glass, telling me their stories and explaining their miracles, assumedly trying to help me "figure it out." I think that she thought I knew less about them than I did (having grown up Catholic), not realizing that my confused expression was more from struggling to understand her Italian.

When we left the church, I asked Signora Bacca if we could drive to Smerano, just across the valley, where I knew my direct relatives on my grandmother's side had lived. She said yes, and we walked to the garage just off the square where she kept her car. The garage door was stuck, so Signora Bacca whacked it a couple of times with her fist, loosening it before lifting it up. We rode for 10 minutes along switchback mountain roads, passing through apple orchards and over an enormous gorge, before reaching Smerano's main square. Signora Bacca pointed out the beige stone house where my relatives had lived, a prime piece of real estate on the edge of the *piazza*, just behind the village church.

After showing me the house, Signora Bacca drove up a narrow country road that wound above the town. A half-mile outside the village, she parked in some wild grass on the side of the road and got out. We were at the Smerano cemetery. Almost before I had a chance to look around, Signora Bacca was pointing out the tombstones of various Reclas and Baccas, telling me dates and causes of death, jobs and family histories—he was killed in the war, she died in childbirth, he was a baker, she worked in the orchards and had six children. Looking around and seeing all of these graves, I was filled with a strange mix of respect and indifference. This was my history, my ancestry, the trail of lives that traced out behind me, and yet I felt no connection to any of these people. I'd never heard of them, much less known any of them. They were strangers to me, only strangers with my name.

Suddenly, I sneezed. Signora Bacca said something, but all I made out was the word *fiori*. Thinking she'd asked if I had allergies, I waved her off. "No, no, no," I said. It was only after the words were out of my mouth that I realized she'd remarked that we all bloom and then die, passing like the flowers.

We drove home and Signora Bacca cooked us dinner. It had been a tiring day, and my Italian was still suffering. I wasn't comprehending as much as I normally did, and my sentences were broken and unsure of themselves, leading to stilted conversations with Signora Bacca and an increasing sense of awkwardness. But the home-cooked food brought back some of my energy, and as Signora Bacca and I sat over her vegetable pie and salad, our conversation started improving again. We talked about what I was studying in school. Our mutual dislike of both President George W. Bush and Prime Minister Berlusconi brought us one of those pleasantly smug moments found only in shared enmity. I asked her how the region had changed since she was a little girl, which she took to mean how her thinking had changed, and she told me how important religion was for her and how she was sacrificing this life for a better one.

Being irreligious, it was a notion that frustrated and confused me and, like her solitary life, made me pity her in a way. I'd just spent two months living out a dream, traveling Europe, flooding my senses and experiencing everything every day. To be suddenly confronted with a life that had been largely spent in a single region and spent alone ... it seemed terribly unfulfilled.

When we were finished with dinner, Signora Bacca

suggested that we go for a walk. She took my hand and led me down one of the thin roads that meandered out of Nanno. It was lined with apple trees on both sides, their lime-colored flesh just beginning to plump. The sun was starting to go down in the Dolomites, and the mountains began to settle into a deep lavender as one peak threw its shadow over another.

Neither of us spoke until we passed a small roadside shrine to the Madonna. Signora Bacca said it was there to commemorate the Virgin providing a miracle and protecting the town during the Second World War. It had remained unspoiled, flawless, an untroubled little village touched only by row upon row of apple trees and the changing pastels of the encircling mountaintops.

I looked at Signora Bacca, who was smiling as she said this, and then I gazed out over the orchards and mountain peaks and wildflowers, and then the little town at my back. Suddenly it was easy to understand how someone could be content here, how one could spend her entire life in this place and never really want to leave.

CHARLIE USHER *is a recent graduate of the University of Wisconsin-Madison, where he studied creative writing, served as editor of the Madison Review, and wrote an international-perspective column for the Madison Observer, a student newspaper. He lives in Seoul, where he teaches English, writes for K-Scene magazine, and does editing work for an advertising agency. He studied in Europe in the spring of his junior year.*

CARTOLINA POSTALE

*Traveling
is almost like
talking with men
of other centuries.*
- René Descartes

LE PIÙ BELLE ACQUE DEL MONDO
SALSOMAGGIORE
PERIODO DI CURA
MARZO — NOVEMBRE

Sicilia
& Napoli

Italy

Pompeii

Napoli

Stromboli

Pompeii

Not As Seen on TV

heather strickland

Cornelia Veneria Pompeianorum was once a bustling Roman city, sitting on a plateau of cooled, hardened lava in the fertile valley of a beautiful countryside, near a busy port on the Sarno River. Since its founding sometime around the 6th century B.C., the city had survived conquering by Greeks, Etruscans, Samnite tribes and Romans. But on August 24, A.D. 79, a layer of sulfur ash and lava from nearby Mount Vesuvius covered Pompeii and stilled it forever.

I learned all of this in 1999. I was 13 years old, sitting in my Latin class, dumbfounded as my teacher projected slide after slide of the ancient excavated city onto the screen. For years after, I watched documentaries and shows on the Discovery Channel, fascinated by the eruptions of Mount Vesuvius and how they affected the surrounding cities; by life in Pompeii and its wide fields lined with crumbled columns, its impressive mosaics and its surprisingly ingenious sewer system.

Pompeii's baths were built in front of the city, just to the side of its main entrance. Inside the city walls, a row of houses lined the road that led to the temples, the forum, the basilica and the public administrative buildings—a sort of ancient downtown. In the back of the city, the high society lived in massive houses with impressive gardens and statues of gods and goddesses. From what I saw through the documentary cameras, the area was empty—well-preserved and restored as well as possible. There were even people fossilized in ash strewn throughout the city, forever frozen in positions of fear as they fled the lava that rushed across the city from west to east.

Six years after that first class, I visited Pompeii. I had very specific images in my head of how everything would look, and I was eager to see for myself what I had seen only through photos and film. It turned out that much of what the camera had shown me was wrong.

The city that looks empty in documentaries is actually full of tourists. They mill around, crawl on top of delicate statues, and throw their cigarette butts and drink containers on the ground. I couldn't understand how people could show so little respect for a place of such historical importance. I wanted to grab them by the shoulders, shake them and say, "Do you have any idea what you are doing?"

Worse than the tourists, however, were those who exploited them. Every available space around the edge of ruins was occupied by a stand where someone was selling a Dixie cup full of "freshly squeezed" orange juice for three euro, or peddling overpriced tourist information guides in every language, or marketing large phalluses and erotic postcards. On my way from the train station to the park entrance, I passed booths of these people who didn't seem to understand the historical significance of eroticism in Pompeii.

A fresco in the baths depicts 16 erotic scenes, including one with two women, and another with two women and a man, both rare in ancient erotic art. They were meant both to entertain patrons and to serve as reminders of important information. One panel, in which a woman performs a sexual act on a man who holds a scroll, looks as if it makes a political statement as fresh today as it was 2,000 years ago. All of this seemed completely lost on the tourists as they scrambled to buy eight-inch phalluses and figurines of people in togas and having sex. It all made me think that those documentaries I saw should have focused on exposing the tourist treatment of Pompeii rather than on its history.

> Those documentaries I saw should have focused on exposing the tourist treatment of Pompeii rather than on its history.

The "ash people" were the main reason I so wanted to visit Pompeii. I just had to see the human bodies made of such fragile material that could last so long. I had been so naïve, I'd always believed that they would crumble into piles of dust if you touched them. But the "ash people" I had seen in the documentaries had been created by pouring liquid plaster into the lava cavities left after the victims' bodies had decomposed. They were not strewn throughout Pompeii, as the films showed. Most of the handful that I saw were contained in a glass case in a re-created vineyard, cleverly named "Garden of the Fugitives." They were blocked by a barrier that gave me only a fuzzy image of how a mother had huddled over her child in an attempt to protect him.

The camera also could never explain the feeling of smallness that living in the shadow of Vesuvius gives you. It could never express the thrill of walking down ancient stone streets knowing that, thousands of years ago, that plaster cast was a real child running down the same street after his mom. After years of watching this on television, I found that I could step into buildings or see mosaics and remember exactly what they were, before I even checked it in my "Guide to Pompeii." Wandering to the back half of Pompeii, where the upper-class mansions and the Garden of the Fugitives are located, I was surprised to find that most of the tourists never made it that far. I always thought that the ash, or rather plaster, people were a sight so synonymous with Pompeii, I'd have to wait 45 minutes just to get a quick glimpse of them. Yet I found only three other people when I got there. I could take my time and let the enormity of it all sink in.

I spent hours winding my way through tiny alleys and arches that I was sure no other tourist had discovered. I stared in marvel at mosaics that had been created thousands of years ago, and wondered if modern technology could ever create something so lasting. Stepping onto the main road, I remembered those documentaries and their re-creations of life in the city, with actors pushing carts up and down the streets. I wondered how the filmmakers could ever know if what they had re-created was true.

Mount Vesuvius itself looked nothing like I expected. I didn't remember seeing a modern-day shot of it in the documentaries (although they must have shown it), so I didn't recognize the volcano when I saw it. The volcanoes that we had learned to draw in elementary school had wide bases that tapered to narrow tops, like the beakers we used in science class. We colored them in with burnt-sienna Crayola crayons, and drew rivers of red flowing down their sides. Whenever I drew a volcano, it was the only thing on the page, which I suppose is why I always thought that volcanoes were stand-alone mountains, giant red-brown triangles that screamed, DANGER: MOLTEN LAVA INSIDE!

But Vesuvius looked nothing like that. Its huge, wide base grew only slightly narrower near the top, reminding me of a beanbag chair that had been sat in. It was so covered in green plants that it was almost impossible to see the brownish-gray rock of the mountain. I recognized it only as a volcano from its flat top, and even then I wasn't sure. There was just too much green for this to be a volcano. It was too beautiful and peaceful looking. I couldn't get the idea that what once had been the top of this mountain was blown off by a violent geyser of liquid fire and burning rock, sending sulfur smoke and ash into the air, then pouring lava down the mountain and into the valleys below, burning away the vibrant green plants and anything else in its path.

A bus runs to the top of Vesuvius, where you can peer into the crater, and I felt that if I could just see it up close, it would make things seem more real to me— the smoke, the lava, the destruction. I needed to do this to understand.

But again, the travel guides and the television documentaries were wrong. The travel guide said I should set aside four hours for the park (the Discovery Channel showed me everything in one hour). I had spent time in Naples that morning and come to Pompeii around noon, planning to take the necessary four hours for the ruins, and then bus to the top of Vesuvius when I had finished.

But before I knew it, it was seven hours later and the park was closing. I had missed the bus and I still had a third of the city left to explore.

No camera or guidebook could ever reveal Pompeii to me the way my secret passageways did. The Discovery Channel couldn't come close to the overwhelming feeling of walking through streets where once-vivacious people died running for their lives. The slideshows and pictures could never explain this place. And none of them could have told me that my anticipation would be so worth the wait; that I would feel content to just lose myself in Pompeii.

HEATHER STRICKLAND *is a senior at the University of Richmond. In her junior year, she spent four months studying in Perugia, the capital of the Umbria region. She fell in love with the people there, even the crazy winos and religious zealots. It was an intense, life-changing experience, and one that she wouldn't trade for the world.*

Santo Stefano di Camastra

The Old Country

nina torcivia

a stunning feeling of emptiness struck me the moment I realized I had graduated and was being sent off—sent away, if you will—from college. All those years, the thousands of dollars spent, the guidance of numerous college advisors—none had prepared me for the scary recognition that I, like many of my fellow undergraduates, was lacking in "real life experiences."

I decided to pack a bag and wander around the world for a while, until I sorted out what I wanted to "do" with myself. The first stop on my worldwide trek for knowledge and wisdom: visiting family members in Sicily whom I had never met, people I knew of only from bantering stories told around our dinner table.

Some would say that I barely qualify as an Italian (ahem, Sicilian) American, given my percentage of blood. However, as in most Italian-American families, a strong sense of pride in one's roots prevails, particularly if one grows up surrounded by manicotti and Sicilian slang. While I wasn't exactly sure what I would find when I arrived in Sicily, or if anyone would acknowledge me as even a B-rate family member, one thing was for sure: This was somehow good for me. Armed with my lifelong best friend, Faith, and two tickets to Italy, off to the old county we went.

After arriving in Rome, our plan was to inch down to Santo Stefano di Camastra, Sicily, via Italian railway. Snaking past endless groves of olive and pomegranate trees, the train offered a dreamy, albeit bumpy, opportunity to visualize what my Sicilian family might be like. We took the long way to meet "the fam," stopping to smell the roses in Sorrento, Roccella Jonica and Messina.

I was pretty sure that a set of distant cousins, who ran a supposedly quaint little hotel, would be ready and waiting for us at the train station in Caronia—at least, that was my impression after the series of painfully difficult e-mails I'd exchanged with them from home in broken Italian. Indeed, when we emerged from our coach, our cocoon-like backpacks wrapped tightly around us, a confident older woman with a blond bouffant was waiting. Sporting fake Fendi sunglasses and a canvas satchel that read "Napoli," she slowly

introduced herself as my namesake, Nina Torcivia. We
bore little resemblance to one another. After a quick tug
on my arm and a pat on the back, we found ourselves
stuffed into her pint-sized car, with her husband at
the wheel. Knowing only "food words" in Italian, and
getting blank stares at simple sentences in English, I
suddenly felt wildly unprepared for this trip.

Finally, we reached the "quaint" family hotel. I'd
had visions of cozy terracotta buildings
wedged next to one another, their walls   **I suddenly**
adorned with regional pottery. This   **felt wildly**
hotel, unassuming from the street,   **unprepared**
cascaded down the side of the hill as if   **for this trip.**
into the ocean, with a marble-floored
dining room, a 180-degree view of the
sea, tennis courts and a seaside pool. Only its name was
quaint: Hotel Zà Maria.

As I walked in, humming Sly and the Family Stone's
song "Family Affair" to myself, I encountered original
Torcivias, looking less like a family and more like a
clan, all bearing slight resemblances to their American
counterparts. The language barrier made introductions
a little awkward and confusing, but a sense of family
somehow prevailed. Despite not being half as prepared
as I should have been (i.e., forgetting an Italian-English
dictionary), I did bring one item of utmost importance:
a photo of my *nanu*. Some 20 years prior to my trip, this
man of dignity and poise, along with my grandmother,
aunt and uncle, were the only other American family

members to visit our relatives in Sicily. Well-loved and jovial, he was a hit with the family at Hotel Zà Maria. During an afternoon cappuccino, I pulled out an old photo of myself with him. Nina's face lit up with excitement as she waved it around, calling over to the table a good portion of the others. It was as if I was suddenly real. This stranger from afar really was a Tor-chee-ve-aah.

On occasional trips to the city's center with Nina and her husband, Pietro, visiting the historical museum, sitting in sidewalk cafés, and walking around the impossibly beautiful town, I absorbed my Italian roots. My weeklong stay was a blur of food, rest and pottery. I learned the ever-so-appropriate words *manga* (eat) and *basta* (enough). While my American family saw me as having a bottomless pit of a stomach, my European family was perplexed when, night after night, I was unable to consume a full five-course meal. Faith is vegetarian, and she had a wonderful time attempting to explain why fish was in the same category as meat.

I have never slept better, eaten more, and in many ways felt more at home, than with my Sicilian family at Hotel Zà Maria. The loud, boisterous family I had growing up in America, the ones always ready to feed me and gossip with me, who met on an almost weekly basis just for the sake of being together, still existed in its purest form here in Italy. In America, deaths, divorce and time had changed that. Seeing it preserved and alive once again here was simply intoxicating for me.

The night before we left, we ate dinner at the hillside home of my cousin Pippo, who owned a beautiful traditional pottery shop, Torcivia Ceramiche, on the main road into Santo Stefano di Camastra. After a night full of family, fresh *cannoli* and wine from his personal cellar, Pippo drove us home and began to tear up. He said it was admirable and beautiful that I would want to meet them. My being there meant that I had not forgotten where I came from and who I was, and they appreciated it.

The next day, as we packed our things, my heart was heavy. I wasn't closer to figuring out what I wanted to "do" with my life, but I did learn what I would need: a strong link with my family and friends, indefinitely. I had taken for granted how much they add to our lives. For this one week, visiting my Sicilian family, I was allowed to travel back in time and rediscover how important they are.

NINA TORCIVIA *is always in search of new adventures to pursue. Armed with a degree in cultural anthropology, she likes to think there is a method behind all this traveling madness. She lives in Seattle but has left her heart in Bali, New Orleans and Milwaukee, all places she once called home.*

Stromboli

Looking for Lava

ben bachelder

■'m a nut for volcanoes. So when I decided that,
▌ rather than invest wisely in tech stocks, I'd take
the $3,000 I had saved during college and fly to Europe,
I chose Italy. Europe's only erupting volcanoes are in
southern Italy. In art history class, I had familiarized
myself with Pompeii and written an eruptive history of
Mount Vesuvius for my final paper.

After spending a few days in Rome and Naples, I
was ready to head south to the Isole Eolie, a small island
chain off the north coast of Sicily. The crown jewel of
the group is the island of Stromboli, spitting fire since
the dawn of time. I was determined to get my first taste
of lava at the summit there.

I had already whetted my appetite by stopping off at the islands of Vulcano and Lipari, but they could not adequately prepare me for what I was about to encounter. As Stromboli came within sight of the ferry, I could not take my eyes off of the white plume of steam slowly drifting from its mountain summit. *I wanted to be there.* When I stepped onto the dock, I just began walking toward the volcano. The quaint little whitewashed town meant nothing to me. It was winter, and most everything was deserted anyway. Occasionally, I saw a construction worker pushing a wheelbarrow full of cement or cinder blocks, but no residents. Had I arrived in summer, I could have stayed with a volcanologist whom I'd met two days before on Vulcano. He gave me directions to a pizzeria/observatory that I could make my base of operations as I scouted around the Stromboli volcano. I even copied down a monologue, in Italian, that I would deliver to the owner of the place when I arrived.

I rushed through the town, seeing no sign of the pizzeria, even after I had passed the last houses; only a well-worn dirt trail, lazily curving uphill past a series of old retaining walls, and revealing views of more and more of the village I had just ignored.

Out of nowhere, a small building surrounded by a wall appeared. It was the pizzeria, and sure enough, a small tower there served as an observatory. But it looked abandoned. The gate to its courtyard was closed, and as I pushed through it, I saw that, like the town, the pizzeria was being renovated during the tourist-slow winter. The dining area was torn up and covered in dust. Tools were scattered around; tables and chairs lay stacked along one wall. It was strange, almost eerie. Behind the bar were a few glasses, some silverware, and dishes. Inside a display case were postcards, trinkets, flashlights and batteries, things I had planned to buy when I arrived.

Inside the kitchen, I found a few unopened bags of pasta, various utensils, rat traps.

Back outside, I climbed up the tower into the observatory and peered out at the volcano. That plume of steam was still rising, gently bleeding off

Halfway up, I heard a huge BOOOM! and saw a puff of black smoke. A warning? An invitation?

the pressure that was constantly building within the mountain, beckoning me.

My original plan was to stash my stuff here and head up to the summit unencumbered, but now I wasn't so sure. Poking around the grounds, I found an unfinished three-room building that was only walls and a floor at this point. One room contained oil drums; another, discarded kitchen equipment. The third was empty. Hmm. I could stash my stuff behind the drums and sleep in the empty room. It didn't appear that anyone else was going to come up here.

I loaded my daypack, grabbed some food and water for the trip, and set out for the prize. The mountain was mine! Up and up and up, closer and closer to the active summit. Halfway up, I heard a huge BOOOM! and saw a puff of black smoke. A warning? An invitation? I looked across the gap to my right. A few years ago, this gap had been filled with streams of lava and burning cinders, and now it slowly slid into the sea. I heard the tinkle of a rock bouncing down and continued on my way up.

The first explosion was followed by another, and another, in varying degrees of intensity, every five minutes or so. Without this indicator of time passing, I wouldn't have noticed time's existence at all. I was in another world. My world. *Our* world, the volcano's and mine.

A few hundred feet from the top, I crossed the cloud line and was enveloped in a thick fog. A whole new dynamic emerged, a feeling of mystery, a macabre scene of desolation. There was no life here, only blood-red sand, blood-red cinders, blood-red rocks.

The thundering from the crater continued. The fog got thicker, and a chill ran down my spine. It was cold, but I was sweating. A nervous breeze swirled the mist around, pushing it up and over the ridges, across the path, blocking out all but the few feet my eyes could penetrate. I passed some low, curved walls of piled rocks, shelters that I had been warned not to sleep in because the volcano could erupt at any moment. The ground lightly trembled with each explosion, enough to make me aware that the ground beneath my feet was there only temporarily.

Finally, I could not ascend any further. I had made it. I looked into the throat of the giant. What I saw was not a great lake of lava, but a valley of white mist. Mother Nature's other arms, air and water, were hiding fire and earth from my mortal eyes. With each cough of the volcano, I could hear the liquid splashing back into the pool from whence it came, allowing my ears to take in what my eyes were denied.

A bit tired and a bit tense, I placed myself on a nearby rock and absorbed the experience. I jotted a few lines in my notebook and breathed the moisture-laden air as I sat, lost in thought. My very life was nothing in the eyes of this animal, this fire-creature. One insignificant spit of lava on a random trajectory, and I was gone without a trace. The Earth must live on, and by her grace I was being allowed to witness the birth of the newest generation. I was her guest.

There is always a time for the guest to leave. I could feel that time coming, so I asked Stromboli to tell me when it was time to go. Within seconds, an explosion, much larger than any previous, rang out. I understood.

As I dropped below the clouds, the sun set, and I quickly made my way down the slope to the pizzeria. Amid these raw elements of nature, I set up my tent and ate genuine Italian pasta under the stars. It was a comforting close to one of the most memorable days of my life.

BEN BACHELDER *was born and raised in San Francisco's Bay Area. His hippie-ish parents (they won't admit to it) raised him to be a free thinker, and his university years in Berkeley reinforced*

242 ITALY FROM A BACKPACK

that. *After graduating, he finally left the U.S. and experienced the glory of world travel, setting foot in 43 countries, including Antarctica. Ben is an avid hitchhiker and is a featured writer at digihitch.com, the world's premier hitchhiking Web site. If you see him on the side of the road in his trademark yellow hitchhiking suit, don't be afraid to pick him up!*

Ortigia

True Sicily

catherine orr

Ortigia is no Rome; it is no Florence; and the locals might very well say it's not even Italy. In summer, the tiny island within the city of Syracuse is a place whose intense Sicilian history and charming streets invite cruise ships full of tourists. But in winter, the streets sit empty, and one can rarely hear a word of English uttered. During this time, a lucky American student may just get the chance to befriend a cheese *venditore*, be charged the locals' rate for a slice of true Sicilian pizza, and bask in the bright February sun next to an abandoned lighthouse.

A passionate advocate of studying abroad, I believe the true treasure in travel is allowing oneself to step beyond a comfort zone, past the sites on all of the postcards, and into the authenticity of another culture.

I spent my first week abroad in the postcard city, Rome, doing my semester's orientation, eating late, jet-lagged dinners and consuming plenty of gelato. I fell head over heels for Roma, and as I boarded the tiny Alitalia plane for Sicily at the end of that week, I and my 20 new student companions were asking ourselves the same questions: "Why are we leaving Rome, cultural center of the world? Where exactly are we going?"

The bus ride through the outskirts of Catania—past rundown apartments, strings of electrical wire and countless oil refineries—was nerve-racking, and bumpy. This was not the romantic image of Italy I had daydreamed about. But this road, winding through neon green rolling hills set against a blue the perfect shade of "sky," was taking me to my new home. In the weeks and months ahead, this same road would become comfortingly familiar as I fell in love with Sicilia.

As my rookie ear had to get accustomed to translating even the simplest Italian phrases, so my American habits had to adapt to this new world. Most importantly, I had to get used to the fact that it was I who was foreign. My stride was different—Sicilians don't walk, they stroll—my accent was funny, and my style was strange. I learned my first valuable lesson not in a classroom or at the foot of a monument, but by watching my neighbor's laundry line. When you have to dry everything outside with the help of only 10 clothespins, laundry day comes more often. I only once made the mistake of washing all my jeans at the same time. For days after, my legs had goose bumps, because, though the winter Mediterranean sun is bright, the air is cold and damp.

I soon learned that laundry is not the only thing that has to be done on a smaller scale and more frequently. Sicilians shop for groceries every day. In the tiny *mercato* near my flat, you had to point to the clerk and ask him to hand you the pasta. Some of my classmates expressed annoyance at these "inconveniences," but I saw them instead as daily learning experiences. I loved my feeling of triumph when I made a successful trip to buy a liter of milk. What a wonder to be foreign and find it an adventure even to purchase vegetables.

What a wonder to be foreign and find it an adventure even to purchase vegetables.

Daily trips to the open-air market became one of my favorite activities. I would breeze through the carts of vegetables, fruit and cheese to the vendors' calls of "*un euro, un euro, un euro.*" I loved being recognized by the *venditori* and greeted with small offerings of cheese and olives to taste. Then, my photography teacher challenged me to move even further past the barrier of being a visitor. He assigned a project that involved spending a series of weeks taking pictures of someone we had encountered in our daily Sicilian life. My choice was clear: my favorite cart man in the market, the gruff-looking one with the asymmetrical face, my cheese *venditore.*

As I prepared to approach him, my nerves engulfed me. I stumbled through a slightly rehearsed Italian speech, asking if I could take some photos of him: "*Sono una studentessa di fotografia; posso farti alcune foto?*" To my pleasant surprise, he graciously responded, "*Certo,*" and then turned to the surrounding vendors of fruit, vegetables and fish, and told them that I was his daughter and would be taking some photos for school. Over the next several weeks, I would stop by and take photos of Mario at work. Each time he would pretend not to pose, but he would place his finest piece of cheese in the front of his stand.

At the end of each visit, he would hand me a tub of ricotta or a large wedge of delectable provolone, and he'd offer me an olive stronger than any I'd tasted before, probably just to see the pained, squished face I would make. On my last visit, Mario tied a piece of ribbon the colors of the Italian flag onto my camera. He smiled and said, "*Sarai sempre Siciliana.*" You will always be Sicilian.

Throughout the semester, I took advantage of opportunities to travel far away. But my most memorable excursion was an 80-cent bus ride to see a lighthouse. One of my friends and I hopped on the Number 23 bus, carrying my camera and a torn piece of notebook paper that read "*il faro.*" The entire busful of old, Sicilian men told us exactly where we needed to go.

I nodded and said, "*Ah sì, ho capito*"—I understand—which was quickly becoming my code for "Huh?"

The bus dropped us off in the midst of cow fields and tall fences surrounding a construction site. It was not far from the sea, and we headed that direction, maneuvering toward it past do-not-enter signs, finding ourselves among abandoned houses. Clearly, these had once been exquisite homes, privy to the most spectacular of Sicilian coastal views. It was a beautiful accident. For less than one euro, we had stumbled upon my favorite place, which forever lives in my memory and my photo album.

On the day that I left Sicilia, I slipped away, too sad to say goodbye to friends. My Sicilian experience had taught me not to be afraid of strangers; to be open to a new way of doing and seeing things. It taught me courage and the art of observation. I found that I love to discover new cultures, and I hope never to be a tourist. Knowing how to travel is not knowing where to keep your passport; it is offering your utter ignorance and receiving complete awe in return.

CATHERINE ORR *is a recent graduate of The College of William and Mary and is pursuing a career in international education. She never tires of sharing her Sicilian tales and is always looking for excuses to return to the other side of the pond.*

acknowledgements

Millie grazie to our contributing writers, including those whose work did not appear in this book, for brilliantly capturing the experience of traveling around Italy; to our readers and fellow travelers who purchased the first book, *Europe From a Backpack*, and thus made the one in your hands possible; to our friends and family for sharing our excitement for these stories; to booksellers who love what they do and put our books face out in their travel sections; and to the people of Italy, for Parmigiano-Reggiano, gelato, and spaghetti al pesto.

about the editors

MARK PEARSON founded Pearson Venture Group after graduating from the University of Washington with a degree in business. After studying art history in Rome and backpacking around Europe for four weeks, Mark decided to compile a collection of the best backpacking stories he could find. So, he created the Europe From a Backpack series (www.europebackpack.com). Also, as the publisher of Dennis Bakke's national bestseller, *Joy at Work: A Revolutionary Approach to Fun on the Job* (www.dennisbakke. com), he recommends you pick up a copy of that book, too. He lives and works in Seattle, Washington.

mark@europebackpack.com

MARTIN WESTERMAN, who has lived in and backpacked around Europe, is the author of *How to Flirt, Easy Green, The Business Environmental Handbook* and hundreds of articles. He lectures on communications and sustainable business practices for the University of Washington Business School in Seattle, Washington, where he lives with his wife, two sons, and edible garden.

martin@europebackpack.com

TRACY CUTCHLOW has traveled in Europe, China, New Zealand, Central America, the U.S. and Mexico. Backpacking is her favorite way to go. After working as a copy editor at The Oregonian, The Capital Times and The Seattle Times, she is now a special-projects producer at seattletimes.com. She has edited several books. She lives in Seattle, Washington.

tcutchlow@gmail.com

other books in the series

Spain From a Backpack

Dive into Spain with these fresh storytellers, and ...

• Trek 600 miles on the Camino de Santiago and discover your inner strength.

• Throw your share of 90,000 pounds of tomatoes at Buñol.

• Lose your wallet, your passport, your entire pack—or maybe just your old ways of thinking.

Europe From a Backpack

Feel your love for travel come alive with 58 fantastic backpacking stories from Spain, Italy, France, Germany, Switzerland, Austria and more!

• Billy Anderson stares down death in Pamplona, Spain.

• Lisa Cordeiro takes a will-work-for-food approach to travel as a waitress at a Parisian restaurant.

• And Mike Riley's desperate search for underwear in a Portuguese market ... well, that's another story.

To learn more about hostels, Eurail passes, study-abroad programs and tours, visit www.EuropeBackpack.com